"If you are uncomfortable with honesty, don't read this book! If, however, you long for reality and love and compassion in your relationship with the Lord and His family, read on."

Sheila Walsh

"This is the kind of book that keeps me thinking about its contents long after it has been read. It is disturbing in the best sense for it challenges the reader to reorganize his life."

Tony Campolo

Finding Peace Under Pressure

Peter Meadows

Here's Life Publishers

First printing, March 1990
Second printing, January 1991

Published by
HERE'S LIFE PUBLISHERS, INC.
P. O. Box 1576
San Bernardino, CA 92402

Previously published as *Pressure Points*. This edition is published by arrangement with Kingsway Publications, Eastbourne, BN21 3UN, England.

Library of Congress Cataloging-in-Publication Data
Meadows, Peter.
[Pressure points]
Finding peace under pressure : when your stress becomes distress / Peter Meadows.
     p.   cm.
Previously published as: Pressure points.
ISBN 0-89840-276-X
    1. Christian life—Baptist authors.   2. Stress—Religious aspects—Christianity.   3. Peace of mind—Religious aspects—Christianity.
I. Title.
   BV4501.2.M4415   1990
   248.8'6—dc 20   89-27737
                                       CIP

For More Information, Write:
L.I.F.E.—P.O. Box A399, Sydney South 2000, Australia
Campus Crusade for Christ of Canada—Box 300, Vancouver, B.C., V6C 2X3, Canada
Campus Crusade for Christ—Pearl Assurance House, 4 Temple Row, Birmingham, B2 5HG, England
Lay Institute for Evangelism—P.O. Box 8786, Auckland 3, New Zealand
Campus Crusade for Christ—P.O. Box 240, Raffles City Post Office, Singapore 9117
Great Commission Movement of Nigeria—P.O. Box 500, Jos, Plateau State Nigeria, West Africa
Campus Crusade for Christ International—Arrowhead Springs, San Bernardino, CA 92414, U.S.A.

*In memory of Jane Watts and Rick Lane—
Two heroes of the faith who God took more quickly
than we wished.*

Contents

Acknowledgments

Thanks are due to Aredi Pitsiaeli who typed most of the original manuscript, making valuable observations along the way and Helen Drain for typing all the revisions in this edition.

My gratitude goes also to all who contributed support, interest, encouragement and advice. They include: Doug and Sue Barnett, Alex and Peggy Buchanan, Clive Calver, Steve Gaukroger, Lyndon Bowring, Dr. David Hanbidge, Leighton Ford, Roy Crocker (for insights on Moses, Elijah and Jonah), David and Madeleine Potter, Dr. Anne Townsend, Lars Morlid, Dr. Michael Jones, Dave and Becky Bellis, and all in the Lifeboat.

*My credibility and ability to survive
as a committed Christian were under threat.
I needed answers to some big questions.*

1
Behind
the Masks

The world's least successful kite-flyer was a Californian whose kite blew into a high-voltage power cable and caught on fire. Falling to the ground, it started a brush fire which destroyed or damaged 385 houses, engulfed 740 acres of land and caused 3,000 people to be evacuated. Total damage was more than $8 million.

It does me a world of good to read a story like that. It reminds me that I am not, after all, the most inept person on earth. At times that can be very welcome news.

But when the books of heroic failures are back on the shelf and we return to swimming through the tide of life, our feelings may become very different. I have met, spoken with and had letters from countless people for whom guilt and the emotion of failure have been overwhelming. Through gritted teeth they have whistled into the full force of the wind of circumstances, assuring all those around them that "everything is fine." But in truth—

back behind the mask – they are anything but "fine." They are just relieved that no one out there *really* knows what is going on inside.

My wife Rosemary and I have shared in that experience. Within months of the birth of our fourth son, surgery revealed that a growth on Rosemary's thyroid was cancerous. Skilful though the surgeon had been, his bedside manner had all the charm of napalm. That experience, together with the treatment that followed and a string of other negative circumstances – including the death of her father – caused Rosemary's emotions to malfunction.

Suddenly my vivacious, highly-competent, outgoing companion was completely different. She could not bear me to touch her; she'd become almost a recluse; everyday pressures turned into major traumas; she was increasingly irrational and unreasonable. In medical terms, Rosemary was the victim of prolonged and severe depression.

We were to discover that few people really understood what we were going through and, of those who did, the majority were unable to be of practical help. Good though our family doctor was, we were left to learn from the experience rather than by receiving early warnings as to what might be on the road ahead.

Someone suffering from depression sees the world through very distorted glasses – which has severe consequences for those close to them. I became accustomed to accusations of being unfeeling, uncaring or lacking in understanding. But at least I was spared the gnawing, emotional toothache that plagued Rosemary. She was the one who had to endure an engulfing blackness in which life held all the joy of chewing sand – day after day.

At the heart of most depressive illnesses is a deep sense of guilt – for a number of reasons. For example there is —

The Guilt of No Longer Being Able to Cope. For Rosemary, this meant that someone who had previously handled everything thrown at her now found even minor pressures overwhelming. Pressures she would have once managed with ease — despite having a growing young family, an over-committed husband, her own small catering company, a hectic social life and a full-scale role within our local church in a program of evangelism with other young wives. Now, when pressures came, there was only the guilt of not being able to cope.

The Guilt of Being a Burden to Others. Rosemary's illness meant that those close to her faced extra pressure, added responsibility and considerable disruption. And she felt responsible. She saw her close friends, family — and particularly me — canceling commitments, rearranging schedules and generally changing their lifestyle because of her. And she felt guilty because of it.

The Guilt of Not Being Able to Change. "Pull yourself together!" "Just snap out of it!" These were the solutions offered from some who *meant* to help. What they didn't understand was that it makes as much sense to expect yourself to snap out of an attack of mumps as it does to snap out of depression. Rosemary *wanted* to change — but she had to endure the guilt and failure of remaining the same.

Big Questions

As for me, my credibility and ability to survive as a committed and active Christian were under threat. I needed answers to some big questions. Why did others, who seemed to face even greater traumas than ourselves, manage to smile on through? Were Christians really expected to remain emotionally unshaken, no matter how hard and often life played a cruel joke? Why were our parents' and grandparents' generations—without all the benefits of modern living—able to cope so much better than we? And why did Christians look down on someone whose emotions cracked—yet rally in sympathy with those who had physical problems?

As I questioned, studied, prayed and argued, the answers began to come. Piece by piece the puzzle came together. As it did, I could see how much we needed to un-learn as well as learn. Light also began to dawn as to our own lack of compassion to those others who were equally hurting. How useless and ineffective we had often been to those who were reaching out amid their own pain and dis-tress.

Gradually there came the conviction that all Rosemary and I had learned should go in a book. The ini-tial idea was to take the dark experiences through which our family had been and to use them as a springboard to explore the theme of failure. Soon I was compulsively clip-ping articles that touched on the various aspects of the subject.

My interest in the subject increased with the dis-covery that Rosemary and I were not alone in all we had been experiencing. As I began to speak openly and honest-ly in churches and at major Christian events about what we had been through, the letters and notes started to ar-rive:

"I am a minister's wife and in thirteen years of mar-riage have felt a failure."

"I have never been able to tell people how I feel."

"Thank you for being so honest—it is like a missing link in a chain."

I have become convinced that our churches contain vast numbers of people who would be deeply ashamed if their fellow Christians knew just how hopeless, helpless and overwhelmed they felt. The mask of "everything is fine" is put on in the car traveling to church and is not taken off until the journey home. The mask protects the emotionally hurting from the condemnation that (they believe) would be theirs if the truth were revealed.

I have become deeply concerned for the many who are simply unable to handle the pressures of life and dare not say so. Those who are all smiles on Sunday mornings, while their nerves are at breaking point for the rest of the week. Those who, in the privacy of their own homes, simply say, through gritted teeth, "I cannot cope."

I am convinced that much of the guilt and sense of failure they feel should not be theirs at all. Many who are bowed down under the weight of failure have the right to walk tall. They are living under a cloud of condemnation that is quite simply not deserved.

Five years after the initial idea of putting my thoughts on "failure" into a book, the publishers were still waiting for the manuscript. Despite the passing of time, our "dark days" had refused to go away; the pace of life kept gathering momentum; and all I could show for my commitment to the book was an ever-deepening pile of relevant cuttings and notes.

Finally, time was blanked out in my schedule for the great literary assault. I comforted myself with the thought that being five years late gave credibility to the theme of failure. But less than two months before I began writing, our darkness grew darker still.

Up until that point, I had only to cope with the consequences of Rosemary's on-going — though improving

—depressive illness, along with the circumstances that surrounded it. But now my own emotions tripped me up.

Hitting Rock Bottom

For several months I had been waking up exhausted, struggling through the day bowed down by a weariness of body, mind and spirit. All ability to concentrate had gone. My nerves were on edge. I would have given anything for someone to put a volume control on the Rice Krispies. Time at my desk often involved little more than rearranging the piles of papers.

As someone who had previously drawn from a bottomless well of boundless energy, it was a shock to be sent home from a major Christian conference, where I was due to lead and speak, to take a complete rest. As one of the conference team assessed eloquently afterwards, "Your lights were on but there was nobody home!"

As I began my recuperation and recovery, a consultant psychiatrist told me, "You are not going to die. It is just that you have been running too close to the edge for far too long."

That painful and personal experience brought a fresh dimension to the research I had gathered, particularly where stress overload could be seen as a cause of failure. Before, I had done my research as a mere spectator—now I was a participant. As a result, the material on failure ended up on the cutting room floor. Out of its ashes has come a volume that I pray will help you to understand what the world and the church can do to aid the person struggling to cope.

If you have reached out to this book while going through some major setback, it does not promise to provide instant answers. But in the months to come it should help put your experience into perspective — or prepare you for the next time!

When socked in the stomach, our main concern is to gasp for breath and try to cope with the pain. That is also true when we are "socked" with life's pressures. We tend to be preoccupied with surviving rather than looking to discover the lessons to be learned from the experience. Let me encourage you that there will come a time when you will be ready to view your experience in a different light. I have a copy of a letter I wrote to a friend at one of our family's lowest times. It includes these words: "Much of the time it appears that the problems and pressures shout so loudly that we simply are not aware of what God is saying to us." But for all of us the time *will* come for reflection — when the lessons can be learned, applied and used.

This book says some strong things about the church, bringing the danger that my attitude could be misunderstood. Let me put it this way: I love my children, yet it is not in their best interests, or mine, to avoid the truth about them. The same can be said for the church.

The church is our Saviour's most treasured possession. He gave His lifeblood to purchase it and sent His Spirit to empower it. The church is now to be His hands and feet. Nevertheless, He has not yet finished shaping us into what we should be. I can only hope that this book will make at least a small contribution in this refining process.

I would have given anything for a book to help Rosemary and me understand and respond to all we were going through in our times of crisis. If this book can meet that need for even one other person, it will have been worth it all. My prayer is that these words will deliver you from guilt and defeat that should not be yours, and also enable you to help others find their own peace under pressure.

God created humankind with all the reflex
mechanisms necessary for survival. Our problem is
that the world we have created is such that those
protective mechanisms are now harming us.

2
Stressfully
Yours

Why do so many of us wear a mask to hide the way we
really feel?

Why do the normal setbacks and disappointments
of life sometimes take on such overwhelming significance?

How come we have trouble sleeping — or waking?

Why do we get so easily upset over trivialities?

Why is it that, at times, even a small crisis can overwhelm us and lighthearted banter gets under our skin?

How come we hit a pressure point and go under?

In answering these questions, we begin to see why
so much of our inability to cope is nothing more than a
natural response to the kind of world we live in. It is a world
of *stress* — the cause of so many of our problems.

The concept is not hard to understand. Pursued by

a raging bull and confronted by a five-bar gate, what is it that enables you to make a leap to safety that is well beyond your normal ability?

The answer is "adrenaline" — one of the body chemicals that floods into the bloodstream at a signal from the brain — causing your heart rate to soar and your muscles to tense in anticipation. An event outside your body (the charging bull) triggers the brain to cause changes within the body in order to make a response.

Remember the last time something or someone invaded the serenity of your private world — be it an aggressive motorist or an unhelpful check-out attendant? Can you recall how swiftly your heart hit your mouth, pounding away before you had hardly drawn a breath?

Your autonomic (automatic) nervous system had burst into life — just as it always does whenever you are under some external threat or pressure. We have been made so that when faced with danger our whole body begins to work for our survival.

This is all normal, natural and essential. You sense a threat to your well-being; instinctive reactions prime you for self-survival; your brain prepares your body to cope.

As you lock your car in the parking garage and begin to move toward the elevator, the threat of an advancing shadowy figure is met by your whole body bursting into life on your behalf. At the command of your brain, a wide range of hormones and body chemicals instantly spring into action. Their role is to equip you to survive, either by staying to fight or running way. Whether you choose "fight" or "flight," the changes your body requires are the same.

The release of adrenaline serves to mobilize the energy reserves of the body. At the same time, blood flows from the outer areas (such as the extremities and skin) and the stomach to the muscles, taking nourishment in the form of blood sugar and oxygen. It is this redistribution of blood that causes someone to look pale and have cold hands, because their blood is busy on essential work elsewhere.

Redistributing the blood causes the heart to pump swiftly and powerfully. This creates the most tangible recognition that something is going on. But there is a lot more happening as well.

Your instinctive reactions, priming you for self-survival, cause your spleen to send out increased numbers of red blood cells — providing extra oxygen and nourishment to the muscles and the brain. At the same time, the blood is made more able to clot, in preparation for any failure to flee fast enough or to fight with sufficient ferocity.

Meanwhile the liver is creating vital vitamins, especially B and C, conveying them to the muscles via the blood. And the stomach is releasing hydrochloric acid, a function normally reserved to digest food. Simultaneously and almost imperceptibly, the body experiences a tensing of the muscles — again, ready for "fight" or "flight."

When "Fight" or "Flight" Is Not Possible

What I have just documented is a perfectly normal and healthy reaction to an external threat. It is a description of the way stress helps us to survive. Why is it, then, that stress in our society is held to be so destructive? Why does the Harley Street, London, consultant Dr. Malcom Carruthers talk of stress as "the epidemic of the 80's"? He points out that in the 30's and 40's the traveling X-ray unit helped to keep down TB, the epidemic of the times. Now he is one of a growing number who take a mobile stress unit out on the road to do battle with what he sees as today's equivalent of TB.

Our bodies were designed to respond to any external threat by taking the immediate action of "fight" or "flight." In each case, the perceived danger was dealt with and laid to rest. Today, many of the issues that bear down upon us defy instant resolution. We are unable to kill them off through confrontation, nor can we escape their grip by flight.

The threats we face today endanger more than our physical lives. There is no instant solution to balancing the budget, resolving conflicting relationships, confronting oppressive air pollution, coping with a possible layoff on the job, extracting ourselves from freeway gridlock — to give but a few random examples.

As a result, no appropriate physical response can be made in order to resolve the situation. As a result, the stress products that have been prompted to flow through the body system continue to change the way our bodies and minds operate until they are eventually absorbed into storage or used up. And while that slow process takes place, the body and the emotions suffer.

The threat of being out of work or flunking out of school might hang over us for months. An unhappy relationship can make us miserable for years. Thus, even the *fear* of being jobless, failing to make the grade or being stuck in a poor relationship will set all the "fight" or "flight" mechanisms in process.

The new vocabulary of the workplace tells its own story: hostile take-over, downsizing, rationalizations, corporate raider, merger. No generation has had such a sword of Damocles forever hanging over it's work force — with each member lacking the resources for either "fight" or "flight." For who can escape when the alternative is to be

unable to pay the bills? And who dare ever dream of fighting "the system" and winning?

A survey by advertising agency D'Arcy Masius Ben-
ton & Bowles found that three-fourths of Americans claim
their jobs cause them stress. In a 1985 study, the National
Center for Health Statistics concluded that more than half
of 40,000 workers surveyed considered they had, over the
past two weeks, experienced "a lot" or "moderate" stress.

Both these statistics are quoted in a *Newsweek*
cover story devoting five full pages to "Stress on the Job."[1]
The article quotes the claim of experts that stress in the
workplace costs the United States economy as much as
$150 billion a year—almost the size of the Federal deficit.
Newsweek added that "the Surgeon General's most recent
report indicates that two-thirds of all illnesses before the
age of 65 are preventable."

The Dangers of Prolonged Stress

We hit problems when the external signals to our
brain are unyielding, when the constant charge of
adrenaline, blood sugars and fats into our metabolism is
constant. Then stress becomes distress—damaging our
bodies and our emotions.

Prolonged stress accounts for large numbers of
physical and emotional illnesses. Physically it can lead to a
wide range of disorders, including high blood pressure,
heart disease, asthma, indigestion, diabetes, chronic constipation, peptic ulcers and skin rashes. Our emotions also
suffer under the impact of stress, leading to insomnia,
tiredness, headaches, nervous breakdown and depression.

The Bible tells us we are fearfully and wonderfully
made (Psalm 139:14). That truth is displayed in the fact
that God created humankind with all the reflex

mechanisms necessary for survival. Our problem is that the world we have created is such that those protective mechanisms are now harming and even killing us.

Our family was jammed into a station wagon, eight miles out of Boulogne in northern France. Without warning, the rear stabilizing bar of the suspension on our trusty auto broke clean through. From being as roadworthy as a five-year-old car can be, it had become unstable and virtually unsteerable.

As far as we can tell the problem began when the bar had taken a hard knock some time earlier. But continued pressure and stress had finally taken its toll. Now I could give the car all the instructions that I wanted via the steering wheel, but it was totally unable to respond.

We understand how prolonged physical stress can produce that result in something like a car. We also understand how marching soldiers need to "break step" when crossing a bridge. But we are only just beginning to realize that prolonged and excessive emotional and psychological stress can have the same kind of impact on people.

The Effects of Change

About forty years ago Canadian Hans Selye borrowed the word *stress* from physics in order to describe the way the body responds to outside events. His work laid the foundation for a new wave of stress researchers like Dr. Thomas Holmes and Dr. Richard Rahe, of the University of Washington, who made a study of the way change affects our bodies and our minds. Dr. Holmes discovered that, "four out of five people who have experienced many dramatic changes in their lives over the past year can expect major illness within the next two years."

The research also demonstrated it is not only adverse events that induce stress. Any outside condition or experience that we must confront, even those that we welcome and enjoy, can cause stress as well.

The result of Dr. Holmes's and Dr. Rahe's findings was the now famous Life Change Units Scale. Possible events in a person's life were listed on a scale according to the amount of stress they induce. The scale lists the death of a marriage partner as the most traumatic experience through which anyone can pass. And even welcome experiences, like the birth of a child or an outstanding personal achievement, will contribute to our level of stress.

Danger comes when we accumulate too high a score on the scale in too short a time. The greater our total over a six-month period, the more likely it is we will suffer from the symptoms of stress overload. A score between sixty and eighty is considered normal. Over one hundred indicates a lot of stress — high enough to increase a person's likelihood of illness by up to 80 percent.

It was found that of those with a score between 150 and 300, just over half had suffered serious illness. Yet the occurrence of illness rose dramatically to eight out of ten for those with a score over 300. And that was our family's experience.

In less than six months, Rosemary had encountered a new baby, the death of her father, a life-threatening medical condition and a number of other "life changes," including Christmas. She tipped the scale at 315. Her system went into overload and her emotions became unmanageable. The result was the most severe of all the by-products of stress — depression.[2] At the time, it made no sense at all. But now, with the Rahe Scale in front of us, it makes all the sense in the world.

LIFE CHANGE UNITS SCALE[3]

Event	Score
Death of a spouse	100
Divorce	73
Marital separation	65
Prison term	63
Death of a close family member	53
Personal injury or illness	53
Marriage	50
Losing job	47
Marital reconciliation	45
Retirement	45
Change in health of a family member	44
Pregnancy	40
Sex difficulties	39
Gain of new family member	39
Business readjustment	39
Change in financial state	38
Death of a close friend	37
Change in different type of work	36
Change in number of marital arguments	35
Large mortgage or loan	31
Foreclosure of mortgage or loan	30
Change of responsibilities at work	29
Son or daughter leaving home	29
Trouble with in-laws	29
Outstanding personal achievement	28
Spouse begins or stops work	26
Begin or end school or college	26
Change in living conditions	25
Trouble with boss	20
Change in working hours	20
Change in residence	20
Change in school or college	20
Change in recreation	19
Change in church activities	18
Change in social activities	18
Moderate mortgage or loan	17

Change in sleeping habits	16
Change in number of family get-togethers	15
Change in eating habits	15
Holiday	13
Christmas	12
Minor violation of the law	11

We have now seen how the world we live in can be hostile to our physical and emotional well-being. But why has the damage reached epidemic proportions? We will take a look at that in the next chapter.

*Today our society faces more decisions in coping
with one load of laundry than our grandparents
may have faced in a lifetime!*

3
An Avalanche
of Change

Why do past generations appear not to have suffered from stress in the way that this one has? Didn't the condition exist? Or have researchers simply given a name to something that was always there, and found there is money in treating and writing about it?

After all, past generations had to cope with outside lavatories, food rationing, washtubs, the Depression, hand-turned washing machines and a lack of all the benefits of our present high-tech society. If they could come smiling through, why can't we?

Our grandparents and great-grandparents encountered bereavement, illness, Christmas, childbirth and the rest. Yet they had no recreation centers, compact disc players, home computers, mail order catalogs, theme parks, disposable diapers or central heating. So if we have never had it so good, why is it so many of us have it so bad?

Of course, stress *has* always existed. But today

there are vital differences. In the past, stress did not exist at its present scale of intensity and, at the same time, the lifestyle of our parents and grandparents reduced their vulnerability to its impact.

The key factor in Richard Rahe's Life Change Units Scale is that of "change." But what it does not take into account is the *frequency* of change we encounter today and the rate at which this is escalating. The damage this rapid rate of change would inflict was stunningly prophesied in Alvin Toffler's runaway bestseller *Future Shock*.

Writing in 1970, Toffler focused on the major differences between "now" and "then." He painted a stark picture of how runaway change in many areas of life will inflict damage never experienced by previous generations. He predicted that the rapid changes happening within our society could only bring a "future shock." His observations show why previous generations have escaped stress but we cannot.

We will always be prone to guilt over the impact of stress in our lives until we understand how comprehensively change has come. Today we face pressure from—

Changing Technology

Today our society faces more scientific decisions in coping with one load of laundry than our grandparents may have faced in a lifetime.

In our ancestors' day, the weekly wash was done in a copper cauldron, with one heat-setting (on!) and one piece of technological equipment—a laundry stick. Today the copper cauldron's successor offers a range of programs from A to N, with options that include pre-wash, minimum iron, cool wash and special treatments. Detergents range from biological to illogical—with or without an added all-fabric bleach. And that says nothing of what we can put with the detergent to give bounce, softness or a very strange smell.

A manual typewriter and a telephone were once all that a complete office required. Today, the personal computer rules; telephones play tunes and almost make decisions for you; photocopiers have a multitude of programs; and FAX machines make sending information as easy as dialing a phone number.

The dashboard of a modern car resembles the controls of a space shuttle. Once, a car horn that played a tune brought the neighborhood to a standstill. Today we have cars that talk to us.

The technology that is supposed to make our lives easier comes with a pressure all its own.

Changing Knowledge

Although the vast growth and change in what we know is stress inducing, the *pace* at which this knowledge brings changes to those who encounter it can be stressful as well.

Knowledge about our environment affects the products we purchase—from gasoline to aerosols to biodegradable packaging. Just when we'd all switched from using aerosols to pump bottles in order to save the ozone layer, they developed an environmentally safe aerosol! Knowledge gained from medical research changes our eating habits—goodbye cholesterol, hello oat bran.

Our first four children came into the world neatly spaced with more or less two years between them. But even in these brief periods, the attitudes and philosophies about infant care constantly changed. One year Rosemary would be encouraged to breast-feed; two years later it was the bottle. Feeding on demand became feeding to a routine. Everyone had an opinion based on whatever magazine article they'd read that week. And that is just *one* example of the way the escalating change of knowledge impacts our lives.

Changing Vocabulary

Writing in 1970, Alvin Toffler observed that in the four centuries since Shakespeare, some 200,000 words have dropped out of our language and been replaced by others — and that a full third of this turnover has occurred within the previous fifty years alone. The escalation of word change has continued such that we not only have a plethora of new words, but many of the old ones have changed their meaning.

Edward de Bono, of lateral thinking fame, brought out his own *Dictionary of Vital Words*[1] to help us keep track of words like *subliminal, surreal, rationale, optimize* and *esoteric.* He also provides explanations of why *profile* is not the way you look side on, *plug-in* has nothing to do with electronics, and *crunch* can have something to do with numbers.

Change Through Mobility

Two generations ago it was not unusual to find people who had been educated, employed, married and buried in the town where they had been born. Today such people are exceptions.

The need to find a home that is affordable, or employment that is available, draws multitudes of people away from their family roots. Families once spent their lives with the security and familiarity of a settled group of relatives and friends. People in the work force would build lifelong friendships with their coworkers. But employers are increasingly demanding the right to move employees on, again and again, in the name of progress and promotion.

Work is no longer the stable environment that it once was. Previous generations expected a minimum number of moves within their career lifetime. The parting handshake, accompanied by a gold watch for thirty-five years of faithful service, was not the rare event that it is today. Employment which offers that kind of security is becoming increasingly difficult to find as well. Even long-term employees are all too regularly shuffled and redistributed to new tasks and locations. Rapid career changes are not unusual. It is estimated that those entering the world of work today face the prospect of being retrained three times before they retire. Others are working on the new vogue of limited contract commitment where, either as an individual specialist or part of a specially recruited team, they will work on a short-term project before moving on to new people and environments to start again.

Even those who avoid mobility change for themselves face the effects that can come as those around them move up, on or out. Ten years ago Rosemary and I were working together with nine other married couples in a program of evangelism within our local church. Today eight of those couples are scattered far and wide. Even by staying still ourselves we have not been unaffected by the greater mobility within our society.

What should alarm us is the way we are building the stress of change into the lives of our children. The mobility of parents means that their children no longer enjoy stable relationships with the same group of friends at their school or church. Teacher turnover can also cause stress — with some children having a succession of teachers within the same year.

Greater mobility is directly responsible for increased stress. And by isolating ourselves from the relatives and the friends with whom we grew up, we are robbed of the help we need in order to cope with the effects of stress when they come.

Several years ago I spent a week in Belfast, Northern Ireland, in order to research a series of articles. The opportunity to listen and learn in that environment was a great attraction. But I saw the highlight of the visit as having the opportunity to stay in the home of the Irish Christian folk singer Rodney Cordner.

I must confess that, much as I like Rodney as a person, my real reason for putting the event so high on my list was that he had six children, managed a busy schedule and still kept his head above water. In contrast, Rosemary and I had only four children at the time and found ourselves stretched to the point of being overwhelmed. I went looking for the secret of Rodney's success and discovered it the moment I stepped into the Cordner living room. There was Rodney's wife, her two sisters and their mother, each with a child on her knee. These maternal in-laws all lived within walking distance of his home.

Our four children had only one mother who was stretched to her breaking point, while these six children had four mothers between them. No wonder Rodney could cope. When Rosemary and I were going under, the problem was not the absence of relatives who cared. Rather, they simply lived too far away to be able to reach out and take the pressure off when it was needed.

Previous generations were born and buried in the same community. Sisters, brothers, aunts, uncles, grandparents and close friends all lived close enough to make valuable contributions to the welfare of the family. The United States Census Bureau reports that in 1970 the average number of citizens living in each household was 5.79. By 1989 this had fallen to 2.62 – including children. In 1950, half of all families with school age children had grandparents living with them. By 1980 this was true of only 2 percent of the population.

Rosemary and I are among the millions who grew up in homes where a granny, aunt or uncle lived with us. That extended family provided the necessary relief during times of illness, pressure and stress. Greater mobility is one of the factors that has changed all that. One of the key ingredients for stability and well-being has been eroded in our modern society.

An avalanche of change is inflicting unprecedented levels of stress today, while our lifestyle leaves us vulnerable. Unfortunately, worse news is on the way.

We have choices to make of a complex and
overwhelming kind that no other
generation has faced.

4
Choice, Choice and More Choice

Ford Motor Company once made the historic offer, "You can have any color so long as it is black." Those days are long gone. Now the options are seemingly limitless when it comes to selecting a new car. Almost any make available offers at least four engine sizes, from economy to supercharge; five levels of luxury finish; twelve paint colors; three interior styles. And there are further options on wheel trims, stereo systems, electric windows and door locks, sunroof and so on. Multiply the range of choices together and, in effect, the car you finally choose could be one of 25,000 alternatives.

When my parents contemplated having a telephone, their decision rested on one issue only—"Do we or don't we?" There was not even a choice about where the device would go—*all* telephones went in the hall. As I write, the catalog in front of me offers forty-eight different types of phones, the options encompassing color, style, memory capabilities, clock, automatic re-dial and more.

Overchoice

The scale of choice and the rate at which it is increasing bear no comparison to the world of even twenty years ago. This modern phenomenon of "overchoice," with its stress-generating effects, has invaded almost every area of contemporary life—just as Alvin Toffler warned. I saw this vividly demonstrated in 1974 when Rosemary and I went to stay with friends in Nashville.

It was our first visit to the United States. We were given the run of the house and told to make ourselves at home. On our drive "home" after a day arguing with freeway traffic, Rosemary instructed me to pull up outside a supermarket so she could run in and grab something for our evening meal.

We were running late. In the back seat our first son, Kristen, was as fussy as you would expect from an eighteen-month-old child desperate for his dinner. Knowing Rosemary would be quick, I duly parked and waited. And waited. And waited.

At that time, the British public's experience of shopping was little more adventurous than a visit to the local Mom and Pop grocery store. On this trip, Rosemary had been time-warped into her future.

It was a full fifteen minutes before this highly competent and intelligent woman emerged from that first encounter with an American supermarket—dazed, confused and empty-handed. She had found the sheer range of choice to be so vast and overwhelming that it had inflicted decision-overload. We drove home slowly, with Rosemary in a mild state of shock, and settled on eggs.

In his book *The Want Makers,* Eric Clark notes that in the mid 1970s, the average American supermarket offered some 9,000 items. By 1985 it was 22,000. And he

claims that one month alone saw 235 new items launched
on the American market.

Overchoice has crept up so imperceptibly that we
have been unaware of what has been happening. It is like
a frog and a pot of boiling water. Drop a frog into the bub-
bling water and it will immediately jump out. But place the
frog in while the water is still cold and it will stay there
while you gradually warm up the water and boil it to death.
We are now at boiling point so far as overchoice is concerned, and we are not even aware of the impact it is having.

When Jesus taught His followers to pray "give us
this day our daily bread," each one of them would have
created the same mental picture of the loaf in question. Not
so today. The choice of bread at my local supermarket includes thin sliced, medium sliced, thick sliced, extra thick
sliced, high fiber, white, hi bran, wholemeal, country grain,
wheat, soft grain, mixed grain, rye, pita, rolls (bridge,
morning, finger, crusty, soft, brown, soft grain, white) and
buns.

Do not overlook the fact that alongside this multiplicity of choice we also have a multiplicity of prices for the
same item. It is a mind-blowing free-for-all when any major
purchase demands an extensive study of the competing
prices — always knowing that the day after your purchase
you will learn of a better offer.

All this choice explodes into our homes via the
television, radio and magazines, every day. According to
John O'Toole's *The Trouble With Advertising,* Americans
are exposed to 1,600 advertising messages a day. Such advertising promotes a level of success in terms of possession
and appearance that we desperately aspire to but will
probably never reach. Our subconscious is left to work over-
time to cope with the unresolvable gap between what we
are and what we feel we ought to be.

The problem of overchoice is not limited to our secular consumer society, though. It has burst into the Christian arena as well. Once Bible selection was simply a matter of choosing any copy of the King James Version bound in black. Check the shelves of your local Christian bookstore today. You will find an almost endless choice of translations, paraphrases, formats and bindings. Who can doubt that any day now the King James, Living, New International and New American Standard will be joined by the Exceptionally Good News Bible and a version printed on waterproof paper for evangelism to deep-sea divers!

Our spiritual ancestors had an almost complete absence of Christian meetings and activities to choose from outside their local church. Today we live in an ever-increasing whirl of gospel concerts, Bible conferences, celebrations, festivals and seminars.

Gordon MacDonald makes a good point:

> Weariness comes not only in the things that there are to do, but also from the incredible amount of experience and information coming at us. I think one can actually grow tired from the constant onrush of spiritual stimulation. Words and more words, sensation and excitement![1]

MacDonald is right, and there is no shortage of that "onrush of spiritual stimulation" — all of which involves choice. Increasing numbers of Christian magazines, prayer letters, direct mail appeals and worthy projects continue to go forth every year.

This isn't to suggest that these things are not good. It's just that there will never be a shortage of imaginative and visionary people coming up with a wealth of good things which clamor for our attention.

Gordon MacDonald reminds us that "most of us

have forgotten the era in which the local Christian congregation had very few basic programs aside from worship
on Sunday morning." How right he is.

The plethora of choices unique to our generation includes ethical and moral decisions that are of greater
consequence than ever before. Moral dilemmas like test-
tube babies, surrogate mother and embryo experiments are
unavoidable issues demanding intelligent opinions from
responsible people. We have choices to make of a complex
and overwhelming kind that no other generation has faced.

Rosemary is convinced that her grandmother went
innocently to her grave without ever knowing what a lesbian was. Today we have to face choices concerning our
attitudes toward "equal opportunities" and "positive images" regarding those with homosexual and lesbian
lifestyles.

Personal Debt

"If you cannot afford it, don't buy it." That was the
maxim of my own parents and the majority of their con-
temporaries. In their day, having a bank account was
something for the privileged few, and plastic money was a
science-fiction fantasy. Almost the only way to get into debt
was by running up a tab at the corner store.

Today the average American owes $1,600 in unpaid,
revolving credit. According to Federal Reserve figures, we
carry more than $600 billion in consumer debt, not count-
ing home mortgages. Personal bankruptcies have also
doubled over the past ten years.[2]

Such a debt load naturally generates stress. The or-
dinary person, struggling to survive under their own debt
mountain, inevitably pays for the stress involved. It is a
price that few of previous generations ever encountered.

Disposability

We now live as a society that continually destroys its permanence and regularly disposes of everything from cutlery to clothing, razor blades to relationships. Buildings were once constructed to last forever. Now they're often demolished within twenty years of their foundations being laid, in order to make way for some bigger, better or more rewarding replacement. We are a "throwaway" society.

The Pace of Life

We have also been called the "now" generation. No matter what it is, we want it *now* and we must do it now.

In business, new technology brings us replies to questions we have hardly sent. The opportunity to "sleep" on a major decision is no longer there. The telephone, electronic mailbox or FAX machine all demand instant responses.

In our home lives, instant action has replaced time-consuming activities. What used to take an hour in the oven takes seven minutes in the microwave. But the time saved seldom goes unfilled. It just soaks up more work and adds to the pressures of life.

You would expect that all the time-saving devices in our culture would have made a major contribution to the amount of leisure time we all enjoy. Wrong! In 1973 the average number of leisure-time hours each week for an American adult was just over twenty-six. Today it is not quite ten.

The way that the pace of life has gathered momentum came home to me on a day when I was desperately trying to get some rest and relaxation back into my over-stressed life. It was only a few months before I began the manuscript for this book. Rosemary had finally succumbed to stress-overload and was taking a complete rest on her consultant's instruction. I had been released from all my responsibilities at Spring Harvest, the world's largest annual inter-church conference, suffering from much the same condition.

I parked my car in nearby Richmond Park, a magnificent parkland where the kings of England once hunted deer, and set out to force myself to unwind. It was an exhausting experience. I had resolved to do nothing at all other than walk in the April sunshine. It was so unnerving that I clutched my camera for security and justified my existence by taking photographs of anything and everything that looked remotely artistic.

After two-and-a-half hours (that seemed more like two-and-a-half weeks) of forcing myself to walk slowly, breathe deeply and stop twitching, it was time for lunch. As unhurriedly as many years of bad habit would allow, I joined the line in the park's self-service cafeteria, thankful that it was making progress at the same funereal rate I had set for myself.

Eventually I came face to face with the young assistant who had been keeping us all entertained with his brisk and effective response to all requests.

"I'll have the special baked potato, please." The words came out as slowly as I could manage.

The assistant took my order and placed my soon-to-be-lunch in a small oven with a timer. He then announced, with abject apology, what he obviously expected to be devastating news: "I am afraid it will take forty-five seconds . . ."

When life runs at a pace like that, it can have devastating results. I can vividly recall a personal pressure point one spring Sunday morning. The previous months had seen me run ragged through trying desperately to cope with the conflicting responsibilities of job and family while Rosemary was extremely unwell. I had been "surviving" by continually juggling priorities, being in two places at once and keeping on the go for every waking moment. I realize now that there had not been any time over the previous months when I had ever completely switched off. As a result, I was completely done in.

On that particular Sunday morning I had left Rosemary resting at home and had dropped off the children at the Sunday school department of the lovely Anglican church we were attending. There was just one problem. I began to realize that, far from being able to join the congregation for worship, I desperately needed an oasis greater than a Sunday service would provide.

The wave of guilt that swamped over me was enormous. Here I was, a Christian leader and speaker at major national events, and I could not face the pressures that would arise from joining my fellow believers in worship. But such was my drive for survival that it took only moments to turn the negative into a positive. There was at least an hour before I needed to collect the children — and that hour could be all mine.

Having swiftly purchased my favorite Sunday paper, I sped to the local Happy Eater and ordered the biggest breakfast on the menu. Never have unhurried minutes been so welcome, nor a "Thank You, Lord" more genuine and meaningful.

Don't misunderstand me. Meeting together for worship is an essential ingredient of the Christian life. Here we find new strength and understanding. But the truth is, one of the best Sunday mornings I have ever spent was when I played hooky from church.

A major factor in finding peace under pressure is to understand what our present culture is doing to us. Then it is a matter of taking the right action. And there are a host of better ways to deal with stress than heading for the Happy Eater—as I am about to explain.

We do not have to lay down and allow
the ravaging impact of stress to jump
all over us. We can fight back.

5
Keeping Stress
Off Your Block

You have probably noticed that Christians are as vulnerable as anyone else to a flu virus, the impact of a bullet or staying out too long in the sun. A radical change comes into our lives through learning to follow Jesus, but this does not include a shield of immunity against normal cause and effect.

Just as we do not have celestial protection against pain when we sit on something sharp, neither can we escape the impact of stress. God designed us to react in certain ways and all of us are subject to the effects of stress I have been describing. So we must find ways to respond and survive.

I do not claim to have professional qualifications that give me the right to hand out advice on how to deal with stress. But as a sufferer — as well as a carrier (!) — I am well able to recognize good advice on the subject. As a result, the next three chapters draw from the work of no less than fifteen professional doctors and counselors, as well as countless publications and articles. Also thrown in are a bunch of ideas that are working for me.

To judge how critical your need for action is, look over the following stress symptoms (remember, they may not necessarily be due to stress):

- indigestion or heartburn
- breathlessness without exertion
- insomnia
- waking up tired
- sweaty hands
- excessive perspiration
- tendency to avoid people
- erratic eating habits
- disinterest in sex
- outbreaks of irrational anger
- irritability
- loss of sense of humor
- "blue" moods
- racing heartbeat
- chronic constipation or diarrhoea
- feeling isolated and misunderstood
- persistent headaches
- lack of interest in life
- unreasonable fears about health or the future
- difficulty in making decisions
- misuse of alcohol
- deep sighing
- muscular twitching or cramps
- lack of concentration
- fear of open or closed spaces
- fear of being alone

If you have mentally checked several items in this list, feel positive rather than negative. You have identified early warning signals that give you the opportunity for action before it's too late.

We do not have to lay down and allow the ravaging impact of stress to jump all over us. Yes, we may face an epidemic bombardment. True, the intensity of unresolved pressures, threats and choices is without precedence. However, you can fight back.

How successful you will be depends on your ability to reduce the quantity of "threat" in your life and how well you handle the stress that comes from what remains.

Reduce the Threat

Damage from stress comes as the result of an overload of unresolved fears. Our bodies are designed for "fight or flight" in the face of threat. This means that an effective response to the reality of stress will include finding ways to reduce the number of threats — real or imaginary — to our well-being. There are a host of practical steps you can take to ease the assault.

- Look for ways to spread out or hold off the major changes and challenges that you face. Does it *all* have to happen *now*?

- Reduce your mortgage or find other ways to lessen your financial commitments. For a definite time, choose to put your resources into "needs" rather than "wants."

- Adopt a "granny" figure who could share in the workload of the home. Or distribute the home stress more evenly. Or both.

The most significant step in my own "journey back" was the decision to hire domestic help from 4:30 – 6:30 P.M.

every weekday. Initially it was the generosity of friends that made it possible. In one stroke it settled my constant and often unresolvable dilemma as to whether I should be at home helping out or at the office getting my work done.

- Lessen the noise of your environment. It is estimated that office noise, for example, creates tension that uses up 20 percent of our energy.

- Avoid creating a logjam of things that need your decision. Far better to have one large forest fire to fight rather than a multitude of smaller ones. You may need to read about or take a course in time management.

What if you still can't get all the work done? Rob Parsons heads up *Care for the Family* in the United Kingdom, an extension of Dr. James Dobson's *Focus on the Family*. Rob tells the story of a little girl being informed by her mother that Daddy would be staying late at the office in order to get his work finished—yet again. Her innocent and penetrating question was simply, "Why can't Daddy join a slower group?" Some of us may need to heed that little girl's advice.

- Aim to define your *worries* and turn them into concrete *problems*. Worries nag away, but problems can be tackled.

- Don't leave decisions hanging over you. If something has to be done, do it now.

- Stop trying to do more than one thing at a time. Take jobs in order and plan ahead.

- Review your priorities. As Jesus said, what good would it be if you gained the whole world—or that particular part you have your eye on—and lose what is really valuable?

- Don't accept or set yourself impossible deadlines. Does

it *really* have to be done by *then*?

• Reduce or even stop all drug stimulants like coffee, tea, alcohol and tobacco.

Accept Your Emotions

Studies show that those who are most vulnerable to stress are those who bottle up their emotions. Be warned: Burying your anger, frustrations or hurts will only cause you harm. Talking to a friend or partner is a good way to let your emotions out.

The psalmist David is not the only one who expressed his anger and frustration to God. Read about Moses or Elijah or Jonah. And God was far from being upset about it. Rather, He was so impressed He even arranged to include their stories in the Bible. Expressing your emotions to God, even those of hostility, is more acceptable than your guilty feelings would have you believe.

Studies also show that those who see crying as only for weak people are more likely to suffer from nervous illness. So be prepared to let it all out. Jesus wept and there are times when we should too. Incidentally, tears actually relieve stress by getting rid of potentially dangerous chemicals created in the body at stressful times.

Be Forgiving

The apostle Paul's advice to "settle your arguments before going to bed" has a sound psychological base. It "fights" a situation that would otherwise remain unresolved and stress-inducing. The Christian concept of forgiveness walks the same road. Each act of reconciliation also ministers to our own physical and emotional well-being.

Cultivate a Fixed Sense of Reality

A notable common theme comes from the advice given by stress counselors and doctors. They point out that each of us needs "something to believe in." While few lay claim to a personal Christian faith, they still declare, "Have a sense of belief"; "Look for something to hold on to"; "Develop a sense of purpose."

These professionals recognize our need to hold change and threat at bay. Today the battle is great because we live under the shadow of the influence of philosophers like Jean-Paul Satre and Soren Kierkegaard.

Have you ever heard the phrase, "It doesn't matter what you believe as long as you are sincere"? Or, "If it feels good, do it"? Then you have encountered the influence of Satre's existentialism.

Without even realizing it, the unspoken conviction of most of the Western world is that there is no longer any fixed "truth"—each of us believes what is right or wrong "for us." Sincerity is what matters, while "belief" is free to change from moment to moment. There is no longer a God who does not change. Only our individual experience counts—which may be different for each of us and alters constantly.

The intellectuals of our day have thrown away the idea that we can really "know" anything in a rational sense. The emphasis is on experience. Unchanging and fixed values are out the window. Moral choices now depend not on truth but on circumstances. The world has been stood on it's head. In the entertainment media, for example, villains are now held up as heroes. No wonder the advice is that we should find something, *anything*, to cling to.

It is at this point that I stand taller, confident in the relevance of having a commitment to God through His son

Jesus Christ. Far from being knowable only through my inward experience, I can relate to a God who has made Himself known in history, in Jesus and in the Bible. This personal God offers me a fixed point of reference in a changing world.

A significant weapon in the fight against stress is to develop a knowledge of and a relationship with the God who made us. Read about Him in the Bible. Hear what others who know Him have to say. Lock parts of the Bible away in your memory. Spend time using what you learn as a basis for quiet prayer and reflection.

Our security comes from knowing God's character and His purposes. Yet there is an even greater dimension to be gained when we move from merely *knowing about* God to actually *knowing Him* in an intimate, loving and personal relationship.

As Ron Hutchcraft says, "Stress was too often dredging up my dark side, subverting [my] family life, and shuffling some priorities. I hungered for a peace that would break its grip . . . and I found it. I found that the pursuit of peace is ultimately the pursuit of a person – God."[1]

It is one thing to know in theory that "God is love." It is quite another to experience personally the strength and warmth that God has for us.

Believe in a God Who Acts

The God and Father of our Lord Jesus Christ is a God who is on our side. We pray – He listens and acts. He is concerned to work out His plans and purposes in our life. So, when neither "fight" or "flight" is possible, it helps to settle the matter by putting it into His trustworthy hands.

We reduce the toll of stress when we resolve our unresolved situations by letting God in on them. Sadly, we tend to reserve our prayers of "Father, please take over" for moments of desperation. The secret is to learn to place the details of our lives into His capable and compassionate hands moment by moment.

Whatever the threat (or threats) and no matter what fear they create, the best place for them is in the care of an all-knowing and all-powerful heavenly Father. After all, 365 times in Scripture, Jesus said "Do not be afraid." That is enough for once a day.

As I promised, there is no shortage of practical ways to keep stress at bay. But sometimes we are our own worst enemy. It is our busyness that does the damage. What we need is to be able to say no. We will work on that in the next chapter.

Keeping stress at bay involves treating yourself as someone with a right to a life of your own.

6
It Takes Courage to Say No

Why are we as busy as we are? Is it entirely the fault of our society, or those around us, or the circumstances we find ourselves in?

Or is a more honest answer simply the fact that we lack the willingness and courage to say no?

I thought so.

There are significant reasons why we may constantly find ourselves at the head of any line of volunteers or why we're unable to turn down a request to make our time and energy available.

We (wrongly) believe no one can do the job as well as we can. On the surface this sounds like an honorable attempt to pursue excellence, but it is often no more than pride talking.

How will the gifts and abilities of others be used to their potential if we're forever running the show? How will others learn from experience, as we have had the opportunity to do, if only *we* call the plays?

We (wrongly) believe our value comes from the things we do rather than who we are. This trap stems from failing to see ourselves as God sees us – unique, significant and of immeasurable worth.

The value of any object has nothing to do with the price tag it carries. The real issue is, what will someone pay? The price God paid for your life was His Son. No matter how worthless we may feel, the fact of what God did through Jesus establishes our *real* worth.

We have also been created with individual talents, gifts, characteristics and temperaments. We are the pinnacle of the creation that God declared as "very good." To fill our lives with activity so as to win the approval and recognition from others is both belittling to our creator and totally unnecessary.

Much of our busyness stems from an insatiable need to fill gaps in our lives because we feel incomplete, unloved and unvalued. A greater confidence in the fact that we are cherished and appreciated by God and others would deliver us from the pressing need to "do" in order to gain approval.

We (wrongly) believe that if we don't say yes, the job will not get done. This is a particularly dangerous attitude to hold within the confines of a church or Christian ministry. It leaves us forever subject to the demands and needs of those around us.

This Sunday school class. That volunteer group. This fund-raising project. That mission enterprise. Each is worthy in its own right, and all claim our guilt-ridden attention. We fear our "no" could put pressure on others, leaving responsibilities unfulfilled, the needy unreached.

So how can we turn people down?

Jesus would have been no stranger to this kind of pressure. As He made His way steadfastly to Jerusalem, it takes little imagination to reconstruct the possible words of His disciples walking the same road.

"Master, there is a village close by where many need to be healed."

"There is a distraught family, Master, where You could bring such a change. It won't take long."

"Think of the difference you can make! It's not far out of our way."

Yet Jesus kept on going to Jerusalem. Does His example mean we have the right to shut out the demands of a needy world? Are we free to always let others carry the load? In keeping stress at bay, are we allowed to opt out entirely? There is obviously more to it than that.

Jesus was able to say no because He had already said yes. Luke tells us that "Jesus resolutely set out for Jerusalem" (Luke 9:51, NIV). Because He knew where He was going, Jesus could be free from having to take on everything else. Only days before the crucifixion, Jesus could pray, "I have brought you glory on earth by completing the work you gave me to do" (John 17:4, NIV). As a result, He could triumphantly declare from the cross, "It is finished"—knowing that despite all that had not been done, He had achieved all that *ought* to have been done.

Jesus knew what we need to know—*need does not always equal a call*. The question is, "What is our own Jerusalem?"

When we know what God wants us to do—and are committed to doing it—we are more easily able to leave everything else to God. That will deliver us from the stress that comes from doing more than "the Father's business."

Few have achieved more in their life than the founder of Methodism, John Wesley. Yet he was able to say, "Though I am always in haste, I am never in a hurry, because I never undertake more work than I can go through with calmness of spirit." He knew the difference between Christian service and the Father's business!

We know we should say no but are unable to do so. Confronted with the words, "Will you please . . . ?" many become willing volunteers on the surface while underneath wishing for the courage to say "not this time." We submerge our own needs and rights under a dread of what others might think of us. Or else we succumb to being a doormat because we're convicted that the needs of others are more important than our own.

Keeping stress at bay involves treating yourself as someone with a right to a life of your own. That will involve a degree of assertiveness and confrontation. Those very words can conjure up images of a shoot-out at the OK Corral. It does not have to be that way.

At the back of our mind may be the belief that saying no is selfish, small-minded and even rude, leaving the person who asked feeling hurt and rejected. We fail to realize that to say no is only to refuse a request, not to reject a person, and there are positive ways to give negative answers.

When needing to refuse a request for your time and talent —

- Make up your mind *before* any request is likely to come. It is easier to set boundaries when not confronted with specific requests. Yet it is not always *that* easy. All too often our mind is elsewhere in the universe when someone descends with their request. Should that happen, at least stall for time, asking for more information or a chance to think it over.

- Remind yourself that if they feel they have the permission to ask, you have the permission to say no.

- Stand secure in the right to make your own decisions, set your own priorities, express your own opinions, assert your own values. In other words, you have the right to refuse a request without feeling guilty or selfish.

- Deliberately speak slowly, steadily and warmly to avoid the danger of sounding rude and abrupt.

- Say no clearly, firmly and without any long-winded explanation, invented excuses or self-justification. It might help to own up to your feelings — "I feel embarrassed about this, but I'm going to have to say no" or "I feel guilty saying no, but that's the answer I'm going to have to give."

- Stick to your statement, repeating it as often as is necessary to get your message across.

- Don't hang around. To do so could send out misleading signals and encourage those who are asking to try to persuade you to change your mind.

Incidentally, assertiveness involves much more than acting on your right to say no. It can equally concern taking the initiative to request that your own needs be recognized and met. Often we back off and endure because being assertive seems an even worse option. It need not be. Personal skills can be brought into play that pitch a middle ground between acquiescence and blurting out, "Blow smoke in my face once more and I'll nuke you into oblivion!"

Being assertive does not mean being selfish or self-centered. There will be times when we *choose* not to be assertive out of a desire to support and honor others or through a desire to help, no matter the level of personal inconvenience. But never get into the habit of always automatically putting your needs last. To do so sounds wonderfully gallant and sacrificial. In reality, others can end up picking up the pieces. Your pieces.

This was my experience. I ran out of road at a time when my own needs were so far down the batting order that they were no longer on the team roster. Being aware of the pressures that Rosemary was under, I felt guilty even sitting for a few quiet moments, knowing I could instead be sharing the weight of five children and home responsibilities. Shaving each morning ceased to be a brief oasis of welcome quiet as I listened for the early warning signals of World War 3 from downstairs.

Even moments alone with God had to compete with the guilt that I should really be using that time to take the load off Rosemary. Sadly and wrongly, it was too often a no-contest with guilt winning in the first round.

I have now learned that, to be the most use to others, I must find ways to say yes to myself from time to time. It is perhaps the hardest battle I fight.

Recognize that saying yes to "this" means saying no to "that." It is a fact that few of us are willing to live by — but nonetheless true: Time does not expand to accommodate each new commitment we make.

Each day remains twenty-four hours long, no matter how many extra promises tumble from our well-meaning lips. That means each extra commitment is a decision to reallocate time. We often behave as though extra time can always be called on. In reality, you can only spend what you have. Time is one of the most precious resources at our disposal. Spend it wisely and remember — you can only spend each minute once.

Saying no is an important part of reducing the level of stress we are under. But no matter how hard we try, some stress will creep past our defenses. Next we'll look at the action we can take to lessen the impact of that stress.

The presence of God filling our life is guaranteed to make a difference, bringing a level of calm and self-control that would otherwise be outside our grasp.

7
Come Out
Fighting

No matter how diligently we may seek to hold stress at bay, some will seep through. If it didn't, we wouldn't be human. So whether it is a trickle or a torrent, you'll be able to weather stress more effectively if you take the right actions and have the right attitudes.

Take the Right Actions

Take time to be quiet each day. Shut out the world for fifteen minutes or so each day. Sit quietly, relax and pray.

Breathe more slowly. Breathing deeply and slowly is one of the quickest and easiest ways to reverse the effects of stress. It is something you can do at any odd moment — and it does make a remarkable difference.

Breathing that is too shallow can induce stress into your system. Breathe from your stomach and not your chest. Count slowly to four or five as you breathe in, then breathe out again in the same way. Use this technique to respond to any stressful situation.

Establish sensible sleep habits. Sleep a regular eight hours each night. Remember that longer can be counter-productive, and an hour before midnight is worth two afterwards.

Eat a well-balanced diet. Eat at least one well-balanced meal each day and include fresh vegetables, fruit and wholegrain bread in your diet. Eat slowly, chew thoroughly and don't gulp your food.

Do something enjoyable. Take up a hobby or spend regular time doing something you enjoy for the sheer fun of it. Going to the theater, reading, model-making, watching sports, painting, cooking, gardening—are all good examples. The most effective time to switch off and over to something you enjoy is immediately after a time of stress. Even sitting quietly with your feet up qualifies.

Rosemary and I joined a local tennis and health club. It was an expensive decision that taught me the truth of the Lord Jesus' words, "Where your treasure is there will your heart be also." The cost of the membership certainly generated the motivation to get my money's worth. This was a helpful incentive to putting the facility to good use!

Surround yourself with restful colors.

Get a pet. An animal in the home contributes to your relaxation. Studies have shown that those with pets—particularly dogs—are less likely to suffer from stress-induced illness.

Practice relaxation. All you need is a quiet, warm room with no bright lights. Sit or lay comfortably, breathing slowly, regularly and deeply.

An effective way to clear your mind is to concentrate on a simple phrase or the verse of a song, repeating it to yourself each time you breathe out. Another is to fix your eyes on some distinct object, then close your eyes and try to "see" it in your mind.

You can learn more about relaxation techniques through books, tapes or from classes in relaxation that are held in many areas.

Have a massage. A good pummelling promotes blood circulation, relaxes muscle tension and drives out stress from the system.

Take time for yourself. A significant landmark in my battle over stress was when I began to schedule time in my appointment book for "me." Mostly I allowed for official days off, taking a break from constantly responding to the demands of others. Before my experience with stress overload I had felt too guilty to take that kind of time off. Now I know that I will eventually inflict more pressure on those around me if I do not take timeout.

To check how much time you are really giving to yourself, make a list of the everyday things you really enjoy. Be specific — soft-boiled eggs, Elvis Presley records, eating at a special restaurant, being alone. When you have ten or so items, check off those you have experienced over the past month. The fewer the checkmarks, the more reason to ask whether you are getting enough time for yourself.

Reach out to friends. Establish a small network of trusted people who can ease your pressure and be a sounding board to give you confidence in your own judgment.

Slow down. Try putting a small colored spot on your watch, steering wheel or telephone handset. Whenever it catches your eye, take a moment to check your tension, relax your shoulders and ease your pace.

Laugh. Not many people know that the British comedy actor John Cleese has "another life" in which he helps business executives to function at their peak performance. His assistance includes enabling executives to deal with stress resulting from change. He says, "A sense of humor brings a sense of proportion. We all know that a problem which seems to be threatening to overwhelm us can be reduced to its right proportions by the injection of humor."

The secret is that humor helps to create a little distance between ourselves and the problem that threatens us. We are able to stand back from it by laughing at it. And laughter does even more.

When we laugh, our tear glands produce moisture, the heart beats faster, the muscles contract, breathing deepens, muscle tension soon eases and our heart then assumes a more relaxed pace. In short, laughter makes a positive contribution to our biochemical, hormonal and circulatory functions.

Exercise regularly. Sensible exercise puts to use the physical changes that stress inflicts. A good workout will literally help you get stress out of your system. It has also been discovered that stimulating the body through exercise causes the brain to manufacture endorphins — natural opiate-like substances that can lift your mood and give feelings of well-being.

Psychiatrist Dr. Desmond Kelly, president of the International Stress Control Society, says, "There is no doubt that for many people aerobics burns up the adrenaline which is produced by too much stress and also helps counteract the damaging effects of anger, which is often a part of depression. I sometimes suggest an exercise bike if [my clients] are feeling angry — within five or ten minutes the anger subsides and they feel a lot better."[1]

A short, brisk walk twice a week is enough to make a noticeable difference. Physical exercise has a long-lasting, tranquilizing effect. It also helps you to sleep in a more deeply refreshing way.

Take your medicine. If things get out of control, or show no signs of improving, seek professional advice. Your family doctor is the place to start. If you are not met with sympathy and understanding, ask to be referred to a specialist. Just the step of telling someone how you feel can do a lot to ease the pressure.

If your doctor prescribes anti-depressant drugs as part of your treatment, don't feel guilty. These medications are not tranquilizers to subdue a patient, but they are a way of getting the brain chemicals to work properly again so that stress management, relaxation and professional counseling can play their part in recovery.

Whatever medical advice you are given, follow it to the letter. One of the great barriers to recovery from the impact of stress is the temptation to give up on treatment the moment you begin to feel better. See it through to the end.

One final warning: Never attack the symptoms without also going to work on the inner causes. In other words, the chemical solution of drugs – or props like nicotine and alcohol – can never, in themselves, get to the heart of the matter. It is rather like removing the shining red oil light on your car's dashboard in order to stop being irritated by it. You may feel better in the short-term, but the problem still remains – your car is out of oil.

Pills for heart pains, antacid tablets to fight indigestion, ointments to ease skin rashes, for example, only turn out the warning light. Meanwhile, the real issue remains unaddressed and – like an engine without oil – you are in danger of burning up.

Having the Right Attitude

So as we have seen, when faced with the onslaught of prolonged stress, it is essential to take the appropriate practical action. It is no less vital to cultivate the right mental attitude.

Be determined. Whatever you do, hang on. The human spirit is more resilient than most of us give it credit. In those months when the dark clouds gathered, Rosemary would fill the house with the sound of Barbra Streisand belting out, "I'll never give up." She made it *her* song, translating its emotional content into her own experience just as far as she could.

Be thankful. Do not let past events or future fears take over your mind. Instead, focus on being grateful. Make a list of five or six things for which you can be truly thankful — no matter how trivial they may seem.

Carry the list with you; stick it on your mirror; write it on a postcard and send it to yourself; tuck it into your Bible. At every turn, use this simple method to help fight the lies that life is all bad being told by your emotions.

Being thankful includes recognizing the positive value of your own sufferings. Be grateful that it will enable you to be more sympathetic and of greater help and value to others going through the mill.

Be continually filled with the Holy Spirit. Essentially, to be filled with the Holy Spirit means being sure to keep a clear conscience before God — submitting to His rule in every area of your life, and asking Him to fill you with His peace, power and presence.

It is from this inner resource of strength that our

ultimate ability to survive will come. Yet, being filled with the Holy Spirit will not shield you from limping when you twist your ankle. Likewise, it will not prevent you from the impact of emotional pain.

The question has been posed, "Can someone filled with the Spirit ever wake up in a bad mood?" It is best answered with another question: "Can anyone filled with the Spirit ever wake up with a stiff neck?"

Yet the presence of God filling our life is guaranteed to *make a difference,* bringing a level of calm and self-control that would otherwise be outside our grasp. Of course there will be times when our emotional turmoil is such that it seems to wipe out the effectiveness of God's Spirit in our lives. There will also be those moments when, without even realizing it, we cope at a level that would otherwise have been beyond us—due to what God, by His Spirit, is doing within us.

"Dad, there is water pouring through the ceiling. Come quick!"

That brief, telephoned plea spelled the end of our small group Bible study for the evening. Within minutes, Rosemary and I were back at our home, with the rest of the group close behind.

Every towel, tray and bowl had been called into play as our four sons fought to keep the effect of the flood to a minimum. Walls were soaked through. The electricity had fused. Everything was chaos.

To our relief, the water was no longer streaming from beneath the new bath installed by our plumber earlier in the day. As I foolishly demonstrated to my offspring that they must somehow be responsible, the water began to deluge yet again. To make matters worse, my phone call to the plumber was met with the insistence that he was going out for the evening and "Tomorrow morning will have to do."

It was an argument that the plumber lost. The mopping up was still underway when he arrived, without apology, to repair his faulty workmanship.

Finally a semblance of peace settled over our dishevelled home. I sat numbly in our kitchen as one of our helping friends reflected how astounded the plumber must have been to meet, in my friend's words, my calm, reasoned and unvindictive manner. In his judgment, most everyone else would have fed the plumber, limb by limb, into the food processor. "You had every reason to be steamingly angry," he said. "Instead the plumber met Jesus."

In truth, it must be told that I am, by temperament, a frustratingly placid individual. But I began to recognize that night that God's Spirit in me had made a response possible, in a very pressured situation, that was beyond my own natural and reasonable ability. No credit is due to me. The difference came from the contribution God made to my life. That dimension can be yours too as you let God fill you with His Holy Spirit.

Be realistic. Reduce your stress and pressure by choosing how you respond to the circumstances you face. Waiting in line for gas or at a supermarket check-out provides the opportunity to fret, be anxious, constantly check the time, moan and generally boil over. None of which, incredibly, will cause the line to move one bit faster.

Instead, we can choose to seize on this unexpected oasis as a moment to slow down, breathe deeply and relax.

Yes, I know this is glib and seemingly unrealistic when the whole world and its mother are screaming for your time from every direction. But the reality is that our attitude will not alter the way things are. As Jesus said,

"Who of you by worrying can add a single hour to his life?" (Matthew 6:27, NIV)

Some people come complete from the factory with an even and placid temperament. Others, to quote Josh Mc-Dowell, stand in front of the microwave screaming, "Hurry!" Yet every one of us can make a conscious choice to accept the unchangeable circumstances that confront us. As the well-known prayer goes, "Lord, grant me the strength to change that which needs changing, the courage to accept that which cannot be changed, and the wisdom to know the difference."

Having identified effective ways to hold off the impact of stress, we'll now turn our attention to the people who are more at risk than others.

*What I do with my life, and the manner in which I
conduct my home, business and profession contributes
to whether or not I am a "normal" person.
The more "normal," the less stress.*

8
High Risk?
Low Risk?

I've got good news and bad news. The good news is that
we are not all equally at risk from the effects of prolonged
stress. The bad news is that some of us are considerably
more vulnerable than others. Two seemingly identical
people may face an equal barrage of circumstances, with
each taking the same evasive action, and one may come
through unscathed while the other crumbles.

How can that be? The answer is that our vulnerability factor relates to our personality type, our gender
and our life-role. By understanding our own place on the
stress-risk scale, we discover how seriously the threat must
be regarded and what action to take.

Your Personality

There are those whose very personality makes them
stress-prone. The American cardiologists Friedman and

Roseman divided people into Type A and Type B personalities. They discovered that Type A is more at risk from one of the most dangerous products of stress — heart disease.

Type A people are competitive, ambitious and hard-driving, and they hate routine. That sounds wonderfully attractive until viewed with the rest of the picture. Type A's are demanding of themselves and others, often very materialistic, and they always seem pressured and rushed. They have a tendency to be critical, aggressive, hostile and more interested in work than family.

Type A people often hide their feelings, run up stairs, tackle more than one task at a time, interrupt before others finish their sentences, eat quickly, focus on their own wants and generally overlook the positive achievements of those who work for them.

Such a list makes for very unattractive reading. Who could ever believe that a character like that could be one of us? So we tend to believe that these characteristics must really apply to someone else. Or else we have convinced ourselves that we *need* to be this way and will somehow escape the damage that could result.

Tragically, our society holds up Type A people as role models of commitment and success — people we should all strive to emulate. All-working, no-playing, hard-driving, winning-at-all costs people are the heroes of our public life and business institutions. Many of us have been suckered into believing that this is the way we ought to behave to be authentic achievers.

But not all Type A's are driven by materialistic gain. Many are equally motivated by idealism. That is how it is for me. Money and possessions have never beckoned, but give me a cause to fight and all you will see is my dust. My own Type A personality may owe something to my father — the hardest working man I have ever encountered. That role model rubbed off. I also get a buzz from problem-solving, seeing things change and overcoming obstacles. In short, I love my work and wrongly find it hard to see time off as anything other than second best.

Type A people may simply be desperate to feel needed and affirmed by others. Often they believe their value comes only from what they achieve, or they are only worth what they own.

Perhaps the most unfortunate thing of all is that Type A's are between two and five times more likely to have a heart attack. In truth, they treat their automobiles with more respect and thoughtfulness than they do their own bodies.

Can Type A people change their personality? Probably not completely, and certainly not significantly after the age of twenty-five. But they can recognize the risk involved and act accordingly. Owning up to the kind of people that they are is the first step. Making a conscious effort to put life into a more realistic perspective is the second.

Key action points for a Type A personality would be —

- Schedule time for your family and yourself, and treat it as seriously as you would a business or any other appointment.
- Don't take work or other responsibilities with you on a break or a vacation.
- Schedule regular creative lunchbreaks. Think about going to places near where you work or live that you would like to see or just find a place to sit

and relax.

- If you are working, use time away from the office as private time. Go into work early or stay late rather than taking work home.

The Lord Jesus Christ had a lot to say about the Type A personality. He told the parable of the man driven by business success — tearing down small barns and building bigger ones. But the moment he was at the very height of self-satisfaction, his creator blew the whistle to call "time." Jesus also made the statement which runs contrary to everything the world would have us believe. He said, "A man's life does not consist of the abundance of his possessions" (Luke 12:15, NIV).

Male or Female

In a competitive working environment, men appear to experience the effects of stress far more than their female counterparts. A key is possibly the way men resist expressing their emotions in a world where "big boys don't cry."

Stress counselor Richard Young of Suffolk, England, recommends that companies wanting senior executive staff had better look more seriously at women. In his judgment, "It is possible that they deal with stress better because they are more ready to talk it over."[1]

In contrast, it is on the home front that a woman is the usually most vulnerable. Here she is expected to be competent. A Finnish study, for example, reveals that when a couple takes their child to an emergency room, it is the wife whose adrenaline level soars the highest. She is the one who regards this as an area in which she should be able to cope.

Britain's social psychiatrist, Dr. Paul Bevington,

points out that it is the woman who takes responsibility for the emotional side of the family—organizing birthdays, reminding her husband to keep in touch with his family, planning Christmas and family traditions.[2] She also faces the stress of seeing her husband get an unfair share of the credit.

Studies show that women suffer from anxiety and depression two-and-a-half times more frequently than men. And it is those women at home with young children who inflate this statistic—with single-parent mothers the leading contenders.

The working mother may experience the release from stress that comes from getting out of the house, but this is too often replaced by the guilt of abandoning her children to others as well as the exhaustion of returning home to start another full day's work.

Your Job

The kind of work we do also influences the amount of stress we face. In 1985 the University of Manchester Institute of Science and Technology did a study which categorized the jobs that are more likely to produce the greatest stress. In the list below, the rating is from 0 to 10. The higher the number, the greater the amount of stress:[3]

Miner	8.3
Police	7.7
Construction worker	7.5
Journalist	7.5
Pilot (civil)	7.5
Prison officer	7.5
Advertising	7.3
Dentist	7.3
Actor	7.2
Politician	7.0

Doctor	6.8
Tax agent	6.8
Film producer	6.5
Nurse, midwife	6.5
Fireman	6.3
Musician	6.3
Teacher	6.2
Personnel	6.0
Social worker	6.0
Manager (commerce)	5.8
Marketing/export	5.8
Press officer	5.8
Professional football player	5.7
Stockbroker	5.5
Bus driver	5.4
Psychologist	5.2
Publishing	5.0
Diplomat	4.8
Farmer	4.8
Armed forces	4.7
Veterinarian	4.5
Civil servant	4.4
Accountant	4.3
Engineer	4.3
Estate agent	4.3
Hairdresser	4.3
Local government officer	4.3
Secretary	4.3
Solicitor	4.3
Artist, designer	4.2
Architect	4.0
Chiropodist	4.0
Optician	4.0
Planner	4.0
Postal Carrier	4.0
Statistician	4.0
Lab technician	3.8
Banker	3.7
Computing	3.7

Occupational therapist	3.7
Linguist	3.7
Beauty therapist	3.5
Minister	3.5
Astronomer	3.4
Nursery worker	3.3
Museum worker	2.8
Librarian	2.0

The reasons for one job carrying more stress than another vary considerably. Dentists dislike being treated as inflictors of pain – that may be why they have a suicide rate twice the national average. Pop musicians and actors face stress from financial insecurity, performance nerves and their own self-criticism. Others, like construction workers, have stress inflicted on them through noise on the job.

That ministers are rated as only a little more stressful than astronomers – and no more stressful than beauty therapists – may create an outcry from the clerical profession! The leaders in our churches do have very distinct pressure points, as we will see in a later chapter. But the low rating suggests that paid clergy have greater opportunities to escape from noise, bustle and activity in order to reduce their level of stress.

Rosemary wondered whether a homemaker (or domestic engineer, as she describes herself) qualifies for an accumulation of stress factors relating to *all* the jobs that they do. She lists them as including politician, doctor, nurse/midwife, teacher, social worker, manager, psychologist, diplomat, accountant and nursery worker. The average rating of those jobs would put her in the top half of the stress bracket just above stock brokers and just below salesmen. The husband who arrives home in the evening and asks cheerily, "What have you been doing all day?"

deserves all that he gets!

But there is more to stress on the job than the workload involved. In its cover story on stress, *Newsweek*[4] quoted a study of race-car drivers conducted by Rick Gilkey, an associate professor of organizational behavior at Emory University's School of Business Administration. He discovered that the moment when drivers were under the greatest stress was not when they were speeding at 200 m.p.h., not when battling for the lead and not when heading for the flag. It was during the pit-stops, when the work-crew controlled things. In other words, when their destiny was in the hands of others stress levels were the highest.

An American survey published in the British Journal of Medical Psychology[5] takes this concept further, showing that the really stressed in the workplace are more likely to be telephone operators, waiters, firefighters, cashiers and cooks — because they have little power to make decisions while the psychological demands on them are high.

When we read that miners are highly stressed, it is more likely to be because their safety is in the hands of others rather than their unpleasant working conditions. When we consider the stress on the police force, it is not, on the whole, due to horrible road accidents or violent people, but mountainous paperwork and court appearances.

What we learn is that someone on a production line faces more stress than the executive manager to whom they report, because the manager has at least some power to control his workload. High demands but with no control — waiter, check-out assistant, traffic officer, taxi driver, mother with pre-school children — means tension and stress. High demand *with* control — orchestra conductor, executive, foreman, truck driver—promises a more reasonable existence.

Even for managers, though, there are stress-inflictors outside their control. Research on 1,000 managers in ten countries[6] identified their top twelve stressors as:

- Time pressures and deadlines
- Work overload
- Inadequately trained subordinates
- Long working hours
- Attending meetings
- Demands of work on private and social life
- Keeping up with new technology
- Holding beliefs that conflict with those of the organization
- Taking work home
- Lack of power and influence
- The amount of travel required by work
- Doing a job below one's level of competence

The type of work you do has a lot to do with the amount of stress present in your life.

Are You Normal?

Finally, the value that we place on our daily contribution to society has its own influence on our stress factor. The late Carl Strolz, former dean of Hertford Theological Seminary, said the foremost characteristic of a "normal person" is someone who saw him- or herself "engaged in a socially useful occupation." Those who are busy on meaningless, worthless, immoral or unethical pursuits leave themselves open for much more stress than if they had a more worthwhile pursuit in life.

It is not only *what* we do but how we *perceive* what we do that matters. A person can see himself as merely laying bricks—or as constructing a school where the next generation of leaders will be educated. Another may be feeding, clothing and changing—or shaping the character and destiny of a human life. An executive may be keeping stockholders happy—or providing employment for many thousands who might otherwise not have a job.

What I do with my life, and the manner in which I conduct my home, business and profession contributes to whether or not I am a "normal" person. The more "normal," the less the stress.

We have looked at the factors that add to the likelihood of you being at risk from stress. There is one other factor that could add to your danger—the church.

It is the quality of a church's corporate life—not the quantity of its meetings—that will speak to a watching world and build spiritually healthy Christians.

9
Till the Church Do Us Part

This book is mainly for those who are followers of Jesus Christ. Not that everyone else is unimportant, it is just that those within the family of the church have specific needs concerning stress that other writers never seem to cover.

First there is the guilt that results from falling under the influence of stress. More about that comes later. There is also the fact that, for those actively involved in the life of their church, there is *increased* pressure and stress. What should be a shelter from the storm all too easily creates a storm of its own.

"What is the major point of stress in your marriage?" This the British magazine *Christian Family* asked its readers as part of a comprehensive survey of Christian marriages. The number one answer was not finances, employment, in-laws, sex or education. The largest cause of stress in Christian homes was revealed as being *church responsibility.*[1]

More than one in three people who completed the survey gave "local church responsibility" as the biggest area of stress in their marriage. Six out of ten couples married ten years or less admitted that church commitment put their family under pressure. Those who had been married more than thirty years saw some relief, but even then one in four of them listed church commitment as putting pressure on the family.

Analyzing separately the response of husbands and wives in the survey, it was discovered that husbands rated finances as being one rung above church responsibility, while for wives, church responsibility came second to disciplining children. But combining *all* answers together put church responsibility firmly in the lead.

The general smallness of British churches is a major factor in overbearing workloads. Across the Greater London area the average size of an evangelical church is around 140 members and this is well above the national average. With eight out of ten North American churches having less than 200 members, there are plenty of opportunities to share the British experience.

British church leader Rev. Gavin Reid, in surveying the results of the survey, put some of the blame on "the schemes of the 'Rev. I. Finderjob.' [Rev. Finderjob] believes that the surest way to keep the people in the church, and to stop them from backsliding, is to load them with work. He has the gift of dreaming up important-sounding jobs and subcommittees at the drop of a hat. Every year at the annual church meeting all the job holders are neatly blackmailed into agreeing to carry on their responsibilities for yet another year."[2]

Couples within the first five years of marriage, or

under thirty-five years of age, were found to be the most vulnerable to church pressure.[3] These statistics re-enforced the relevance of children under school age to the whole problem.

The blame for this high level of stress cannot all be laid at the door of over-zealous or unthinking local church leaders. There is also a plethora of husbands and wives who "escape" from family responsibilities under the disguise of spiritual activity. Sitting on church committees is more enjoyable and fulfilling than coping with unruly children at bedtime. No amount of sympathy is enough for the wife who finds herself screaming at her man, "Johnny's sick, the grass is six inches deep, the washing machine has spewed water all over the kitchen floor and you tell me you are going to the *!#! deacons meeting!" Or how about the husband who only sees his wife as she is leaving the house to attend yet another church committee meeting?

Particularly vulnerable to over-commitment are couples who have grown up through the church and now find themselves with a young family. Before the arrival of their days of diaper rash and teething gel, they were free to spend many hours in church activity. Now they are expected — and feel compelled — to maintain the same work-rate without any consideration for their new responsibilities as parents. Moreover, everyone else around them seems to be coping with their workload — surely they can as well.

Added to the work overload factor is the stress that comes from the guilt of having divided loyalties. The homemaker-wife who sees her zealous husband bolt his meal and dash off to save the world feels guilty over the resentment she feels for being abandoned. She loves God, wants to serve Him, and wants her husband to serve Him too. But she wants "him" — and feels so incredibly guilty for resenting the times when she is left literally holding the baby while he is out being busy for God. She longs for his time, his touch and his undivided attention.

This husband is on the rack, stretched between his commitment to his family and his promises to "the deacons." "They" will never understand if he doesn't deliver to their level of expectation. So "she" will have to understand — and make the adjustments when he is not there.

"I shouldn't feel like this, should I?" asks the husband who is a little angry that his wife has just agreed to take charge of the annual women's retreat on top of her responsibilities to two church committees. How can he ask for the time, attention and intimacy for which he longs if it would mean preventing her from "doing God's work"? He feels guilty because he needs his wife as much as, if not more, than the church does.

The Christian couple is often torn trying to serve the demands of two masters — their commitment within the church and their responsibility to their family.

I realize that there is a danger in speaking out like this: It actually puts the over-committed at risk. For every over-stretched church member there are probably a score or more who are shirking responsibility and will use these words as justification for staying that way.

I also don't want to imply that the workload in our churches should fall on the shoulders of singles, couples without children and those whose offspring have left the nest. It is these categories — particularly the singles — who already are too quickly dumped on with every new responsibility and project that emerges.

I write with the experience of the needs of someone who is married and with children. But vulnerability to stress is not exclusive to this segment of society.

Part of our problem is that the programs of many of our churches are just too full. We expend energy in maintaining activities that are seldom evaluated for their genuine effectiveness. We work and plan with a subconscious false belief that our local church consists of the activities it undertakes and the buildings it maintains, rather than the relationships that exist.

It is the quality of a church's corporate life — not the quantity of its meetings — that will speak to a watching world and build spiritually healthy Christians.

What the church needs is an assessment at the local level of what should realistically be expected in terms of workload and commitment — and the support that is required in order to enable it to happen. It is worth remembering that eight out of every ten U.S. churches have two hundred members or less. For them to survive means a much greater involvement of their members than is needed in larger churches.

Unholy Demands

It is not only the pressure on its workers that results in the church generating stress for so many people. But it is also the demands to toe the line on a host of man-made rules and traditions, many of which are disguised as having the authority of God when they have no such thing at all. In the environment of almost every local church there is a set of spoken and unspoken "rules" and expectations. Such "rules" create tremendous amounts of stress.

A classic edict for many churches is the twice-on-Sunday demand. It is the benchmark of "real commitment" for them, despite the fact that it has no basis in the Bible — as has no other official "meetings to be attended" quota.

Rosemary and I moved to our present London suburb as newlyweds and joined a live church close to our home. Eight years later we had amassed our first four children and a considerable commitment as leaders of an effective outreach to other married couples. Throughout that time we had maintained, with a few shaky interludes, the demanded quota of twice-on-Sunday and once-on-Wednesday attendance.

Gradually Rosemary's increasing ill-health made it less realistic to keep all the balls in the air at the same time. So the family was put first. I would like to think that what happened next is not typical in either the British or U.S. church life, and it's probably not. But I fear the underlying attitudes are all too typical. We found ourselves facing the church leaders who were expressing their concern over our "bad attendance," with an emphasis on my regular absence on Sunday evenings.

To have walked out of our home at 6:15 P.M. on a Sunday would have abandoned Rosemary, with nerves unravelled at the ends, to the mercies of four marauding children all under the age of seven. So I was staying put and pitching in.

"Wrong," I was told. "Your responsibility is to be in church as a witness to the non-Christians to whom you are reaching out. Your place is to sit under the Word of God." The scolding came with no practical offer of help to make that unrealistic and inhumane demand possible.

That may sound like an attitude from some heavy handed sect or extreme denomination. In fact, it came from an outgoing independent evangelical church, with the reputation for good Bible teaching and a strong commitment to evangelical truth.

Since that time I have spoken with countless people

who have been victims of that kind of unrealistic, unreasonable and uncaring attitude. They may have had no
direct confrontation of the kind that we experienced, but
they still felt the pressure to toe the line. The issue was not
always Sunday evenings, but were a range of other responsibilities. They have found themselves squeezed and
hurting through trying to live up to the expectations and
demands placed on them.

The demand of public attendance is matched by the
demand for private devotions. "You must read the Bible
every day," is the standard. We try—and suffer the stress
of not succeeding. Yet we have been battling to match a
standard that is nowhere to be found in the Bible itself.
How could it be when, for the first fifteen centuries of the
Church, Christians didn't have their own personal copy of
the Bible to read?

Yes, I do count personal Bible reading as important,
valuable and beneficial. But not to read the Bible every day
is not to fail God or ourselves. It is just "not to read the
Bible every day." Jesus doesn't demand it; the first Christians didn't do it; and no one has the right to make it a
pressure point for anyone else. After all, what does such an
expectation have to say to more than half the world's
population who cannot read?

There are also demands (often implied rather than
spoken) that true discipleship means abandoning normal
social and recreational life. "The devil finds work for idle
hands to do," was the watchword of a past spiritual generation, and it is a view that has not gone away. The point is
made by reading into the New Testament that Jesus and
His disciples never stopped for breath or the Palestinian
equivalent of a game of tennis. "Would Jesus have played
golf?" is one question I have had to field from a sincere
senior saint. And too casual a reading of the New Testa-

ment can inflict guilt feelings on those crying out for a recreational oasis.

We must measure the lifestyle of Jesus and His disciples against the way life was lived in Bible times — not in the twentieth century. As Gordon MacDonald points out:

> When He went from town to town with His disciples, He moved on foot (or in a boat). There were long hours of quietness in the countryside on those walks. It wasn't the frantic jetting around — breakfast in Jerusalem, lunch in Damascus and supper in Antioch.[4]

You will also find Jesus taking time for long relaxed meals, weddings, breakfast with His friends. And Paul had no sense of guilt over taking time to wait in a city to be joined by his companions (Acts 17:16).

MacDonald underlines the fact that "the pace of life in Jesus' time was automatically governed not by inner discipline but by practical obstacles that we have overcome by high-speed transportation, telephone and organizational technique." He adds, "If there were spaces in our calendars created by a slow pace of life, then we would not need to talk about artificial means of recreation, quietness and restoration."

All too often we face demands of performance that do not represent the desires of a loving Father God, and which frequently do little more than feed the egos of the leadership by keeping the numbers up, the programs going and everything rolling on in ship-shape fashion. That can create nothing other than stress.

It has to be said that churches from newer traditions tend to treat their family members with more realism — both in their caring structures and practical demands. Older churches appear to do less well, for a number of reasons.

The leadership of long-established churches tends to be older. By leadership I do not mean merely the minister, but the total lay leadership. I also observe — though I have no research to back me up — that there is a greater likelihood for people to be deacons if they have relatives within their church. These two factors — age and relationships — create a body of people who do not easily understand the pressures on today's family because they have not shared the experience of greater mobility or of being geographically separated from close friends or family.

The confrontation that Rosemary and I had with our church leadership over our Sunday-evening "AWOL" was a distressing event. Casting my mind back to the suburban room where it took place, I can recall only about eight of the deacons and elders who were present. Of these, at least six had close family living within a few miles, while five had brothers, sisters or parents actually within the church. They could therefore be forgiven for their lack of understanding of the pressures faced by a couple adrift from their kith and kin.

The second reason why long-established churches seem to do less well in this respect are the role models that exist within them. We learn what kind of standards and behavior are appropriate in life from the examples set by those who are older or in authority. Much of this learning is subconscious but it is a key factor of the development of us all.

The way I spend my time, the way I treat my wife, the value I place on other people, the priorities I hold important — all teach my children what is normal, right and expected. If I chain Rosemary to the kitchen sink and spurn any household chores, our children are likely to model their own future actions and attitudes on what they have seen. One of the reasons that so many people today struggle with parenting is that they had such poor role models from which to learn.

Our role models within the local church may well be those who are putting unreasonable demands on their own families, who are out when they should be in, and who, themselves, are the victims of spiritual blackmail. But they are the people respected and lauded — and we too readily model our behavior on theirs, as the succeeding generation will do on ours. And everyone will pay the price.

There is a world of difference between self-sacrifice through genuine discipleship and the actions of those who constantly take their partners, or their parents, for granted (or are pressured by their church into doing so). Forsaking everything for the sake of Jesus and the gospel must go hand in hand with Paul's command that husbands should love their wives to the same measure that Jesus loves the church (Ephesians 5:25).

John Mallison is a Bible teacher and small-group expert. He tells the story of being at a retreat for ministers in his native Australia. Those present were divided into groups in order to share in a relational Bible study on the parable of the Good Samaritan. The idea was that each person would try to identify with a character in the parable, explaining what they learned from trying to get inside that person's skin.

One by one the group went through the various characters — the priest, the Levite, the Samaritan, the innkeeper. They may even have done the donkey for all I know. The session was all but finished and about to break up when John pulled them back together. "There is one person we failed to look at," he protested. "What about the robbers?"

God had been convicting John at the very deepest level. That robber was just like him. He had robbed his wife and his family of himself and his time — with the service of God used as justification.

John went back to his conference center room and wrote separate letters of apology and repentance to his wife and family. His wife told him afterwards, "Only the Holy Spirit could have revealed that to you." We need that kind of revelation in our families and our churches if we are to free countless Christian wives and husbands from a burden of stress and guilt that should not be theirs.

Church overload is not exclusive to those who are married, although they do seem to be those most trapped by it. Others affected are the "can't-say-no" brigade (see page 55) and the Type A personality who use their church as the stage on which to feed their emotional needs (see page 74).

How to Make Stress

With stress being the epidemic of the 90s, your church will most probably want all that it can get. After all, why should you miss out when everyone else is getting theirs? So here is a tongue-in-cheek guide to help any church hit the stress-heights. Put the following simple action plan to work and no one need miss out.

To inflict the maximum amount of damage on the greatest number of people in the shortest time, here is what you do:

1. Make sure your church leaders keep their attention focused on high-priority issues such as what the choir should wear or what color carpet to lay. This will enable them to avoid ever admitting that anyone — particularly themselves — is at risk from prolonged stress. Above all, never allow consideration to be given to the level of stress generated for people who are totally committed within a

church fellowship.

2. Continue to bemoan the fact that responsibility within the church is always left by the many to the few, and that the majority keep their heads down and merge with the furniture. Such discussion usefully distracts everyone from seeking practical ways to share the workload on a more even basis, especially if it would mean some things going undone.

3. Avoid setting definable goals and objectives that would enable activities to be evaluated. This will effectively keep people from having a sense of responsibility, purpose and ownership — keeping them on a maintenance treadmill.

4. Never, repeat never, close anything down. This rule holds good no matter how long something has been in place or how irrelevant it now is. Remember the Gaslight Principle and apply it rigorously.

Note: Those unfamiliar with the Gaslight Principle will be helped by knowing that the British 6:30 P.M. Sunday service began as a result of the invention of interior gaslighting. This form of illumination became such a spectacle that great crowds would gather to see it.

Fashionable churches seized on the opportunity to install their own gaslighting and to preach the gospel to the gathered assembly. Starting at 6:30 P.M. meant that the primarily agricultural community could still be in bed in time to rise refreshed for their daily chores. The result — the tradition of an evangelistic Sunday evening service at 6:30 P.M. — still going strong in many churches to this day.

The Gaslight Principle demands that, should anyone ever notice that few of today's churches use gaslight, or that if they did it would be rather less than a spectacle, or that most of those in church are not agricultural workers, you must immediately change the subject. The Gaslight Principle is guaranteed to maintain meeting overload in any well-established church.

5. Make sure that church leaders treat everyone as though their stress levels were identical. This will make it unnecessary to compile a list of those who are vulnerable to stress and without close relatives or friends within easy reach. Should such a list be inadvertently made, ignore it. Certainly never allow pastoral resources to be used to care for those most at risk.

6. When severe illness or bereavement comes to a family of the church, apply the Six Week Rule. This rule means that after six weeks you follow the well-established pattern of leaving the family to fend for themselves. Either assume that they are now fully recovered, or count on the law of averages to produce someone else with a more urgent claim on your time.

An effective way of maintaining the Six Week Rule is to encourage church members to love their *neighbors* rather than their *neighbor*. This is an excellent tactic which spreads their resources widely and induces burnout.

7. When faced with someone debilitated through stress, always ask, "What can I do?" You can be sure that the reply will be "Nothing," because those swamped by stress are generally unable to make practical suggestions as to how others can come to their aid. They also wish to avoid adding to their sense of failure and guilt by asking for help.

Never arrive at their door to announce, "I've come for your ironing" or "We would like to take the children for the day" or "John and I will babysit so that you can both get out for a break." This would be thoroughly counter-productive to the task in hand — it could actually relieve stress.

8. Do not allow the church leadership to spend time together discussing the question, "How can our fellowship be seen to be the church at the times when it is not meeting together?" This is by far the most dangerous question that any church can ask of itself.

9. Jesus told parables about counting your bricks before you start to build and counting your soldiers before you go to war (Luke 14:28-32). But never consider His teaching relevant to a church planning for growth, as you may then take account of the consequent stress laid on the members.

It is comforting to consider that in all the current vogue of church-growth conferences and books, hardly anything is ever said about the way this could impact the personal lives of those committed to carry out the plans.

10. Use the now well-proven methods to make sure that home groups are run effectively without becoming vulnerable to attacks of openness and honesty. This is not at all difficult, as thousands have already discovered.

The key is to make sure that each group is always kept just large enough so real intimacy is unable to take place. A group of less than twelve will always be at risk. The leadership of the group must set an example in maintaining a level of superficiality and avoiding personal honesty, while the group must hardly ever meet on a social basis.

11. Anyone preaching must disregard the fact that the major question for most of those listening is, "How can I get through Monday?" Instead, the preacher must press on in explaining the significance of badger skins on the tabernacle, or any other subject which will suitably convince the congregation of how much he learned at theological college and how hard he studied during the week.

12. Do your utmost to ignore the assertion of Gordon Mac-Donald that, "Many churches are fountains gone dry. Rather than being springs of life-giving energy that cause people to grow and delight in God's way they become sources of stress."[5] And should this truth catch your eye, steadfastly ignore it. After all, there can be a greater sense of fulfillment in helping the wounded rather than keeping them from being hurt in the first place.

Workload may seem to be the major means of handing out stress within a church. But I believe an even greater culprit is the lack of honesty that marks so many of our church relationships.

If we believe the lie that Christians do not have problems, we are going to be inflicted with the stress of guilt when reality strikes.

10
The Sunday
Lie-In

The Western Church must stand condemned for denying its members the right to have problems. Perhaps *the* greatest pressure point of all is that those who follow Christ are expected to cope with whatever life throws at them.

It has been said that there are "liars, damned liars and politicians." True or not, there are probably more lies told in the ten minutes after a Sunday service in most of our churches than in a whole week within the hallowed halls of Congress. Let's listen to the all-too typical "Sunday Lie-In":

"Hello, Barbara, how are you?"

"Fine, Julie, fine. And how are you?"

"Fine. And you, Tom?"

"Fine. Just fine. How are you this morning, Stephen?"

"Oh, fine. Really fine."

Now let's listen again and add what may *really* have been going on in the minds of those involved.

"Hello, Barbara, how are you?" (*I've got to hurry to fix lunch.*)

"Fine, Julie, fine." (*Except for three sleepless nights with baby James, a huge argument with Mike — again — and a panic attack in K Mart.*) "And how are you?"

"Fine." (*Thank goodness she doesn't know what I'm really thinking. She'd have a fit.*) "And you, Tom?"

"Fine. Just fine." (*If I told her even half, it would be around this place faster than headlice at a nursery school.*) "How are you, Stephen?"

"Oh, fine, really fine." (*If you really care, where have you been all week while life has been kicking me in the teeth?*)

It is the assessment of the Rev. Bill Burnett, the former Bishop of Cape Town, that "our dishonesty stems from our desire to keep up the appearance of adequacy."

We have become so preconditioned to the anticipated answer that even telling the truth does not always solve the problem. I myself have responded to a "How are you?" with "Pretty desperate," only to receive a smile and the reply, "Oh, good, praise the Lord!"

Rosemary remembers receiving a phone call from a very dear friend concerned to see how she was while I was away for several days. Rosemary blurted out how difficult things had been and how bad she was feeling. When Rosemary paused for breath, the caller came back with the pre-programmed reply, "Oh, good!"

There are ways to break the mold. I have discovered

that the perfect unnerving reply to the "How are you?" question is, "Just about the same." This produces a wonderful disorientation when people realize they ought to know how you were the last time they asked!

A more positive approach is to reply "That's a big question. If you really want to know, come over for coffee and I will tell you." That method will probably not bring floods of people to your door. The reason is simple: "How are you?" really means nothing more significant than "Good morning." So the lies being told in church have as much to do with the question as they do with the answers. We don't *really* want to know how people are because an honest answer has implications for us that we may want to avoid.

This is not a new phenomenon. The apostle Paul had to tell the early Christians to "bear one another's burdens" (Galatians 6:2). If it had been happening naturally within the church, he wouldn't have needed to give the command.

Pretending Pastors

The Sunday "cover up" is not limited to the casual conversations after the service. It is equally present in the pulpit. Can you remember the last time you heard the preacher honestly share his own problems, needs, hurts or failings — if ever? We are back to the "role model" principle again. If the minister, the example of "true spirituality," never has problems, then obviously we shouldn't either. We become victims of his conspiracy of silence.

A psychiatrist conducted a random telephone survey of a hundred American clergymen selected from various denominations. One in five clergymen revealed that they have had moderate to severe depression at some time in their lives. Yet how often do we hear that truth revealed publicly from the ministers themselves?

Dishonesty at leadership level is a major burden inflicted on everyone else. One of my favorite cartoons comes from *Leadership* magazine. A wife is applying a clothes brush to the jacket of her minister husband as he is about to leave home for church. She is saying, "Suppose you do it the other way around for a change today, dear. Be nice at home and ratty at church."

That kind of honesty is essential if we are to lift unrealistic burdens from the shoulders of hurting people. We need those at leadership level who are not only willing to open up the Bible, but also to open up themselves. Otherwise, the minister's study can easily become a refuge from reality, and "professionalism" an escape from humanness.

Believing a Lie

If we believe the lie that Christians do not have problems, we are going to be inflicted with the stress of guilt when reality strikes. Instead of looking for help or being honest about how things are with us, we will struggle along—fallen and defeated.

This is a terrible burden for people to bear. Rosemary discovered that to her cost. Everything within the environment of our church proclaimed, "Christians do not have problems." As a result, she could not bring herself to admit she was taking medication for her depression. It was almost three months before I knew the truth. She felt so guilty at having problems and not being able to cope. Everywhere else, people with bigger hills to climb were saying "Fine, I'm fine," smiling and getting by. So she told herself she ought to be able to manage with her own resources.

The church sends out a signal to its members telling us we should not have problems because there are spiritual answers and resources to cope with anything and everything that may come our way. This is typified in an advertisement I cut out of a magazine, promoting a book with the promising title, *How to Overcome Anything!* The fact that the advertisement bore an endorsement from the defrocked TV evangelist Jim Bakker is possibly the most articulate comment that could be made on the subject.

Someone I know well answered his office telephone to hear the voice of his obviously distressed wife. He wasn't unduly surprised, because the children had been acting up of late and, to top it all, her cloud of depression had not shifted for days. But all this was not the cause of his wife's distress. He learned that earlier in the day a loyal and well-meaning friend had stopped by for coffee and brought with her a determination to do something to help. Her contribution was to leave behind a hand-written Bible verse tacked above the sink. It promised, "I can do all things through Christ who strengthens me" (Philippians 4:13).

Now, at one end of the phone was a poor woman who had her world caving in around her, not a piece of practical help around, nor a relative within thirty miles. And staring her in the face was a Bible verse telling her she ought to be able to cope. Christ's strength was all she needed. Her friend's loving action, which was meant to open a window to heaven and to survival, had become a pit to disaster. Far from providing liberation and encouragement, that verse brought condemnation and defeat.

Doesn't Scripture tell us that we can do all things through Christ's strength? If your answer is yes, let me ask you another question. Can you juggle? If not, please take four oranges. No, make that eggs. Begin to juggle, repeating that verse of Scripture to yourself and trusting entirely in Christ to give you the strength to see you through.

Now take a few moments to clean up and read on.

Of course, that verse of Scripture has nothing to do with juggling eggs — or eating fire, holding your breath for ten minutes, or memorizing the works of Shakespeare backwards. Nor does it have anything to do with having the ability to cope with unreasonable demands or circumstances. Like every verse of Scripture, it cannot be dragged out of its context, because that makes it say something different from what was intended.

When the apostle Paul wrote those words, it was in the context of saying, "I have known what it is to have too much and I have known what it is not to have enough. I can accept having more than I need, and I can accept having less than I need." Paul goes on to say, "In every situation I have learned to be content. I can do all things through Christ, who strengthens me."

That is the context. He is talking about coping with the need to have the right attitude. That is something very different from holding up the verse as a cure-all for every overwhelming situation. Sadly, we misuse this verse constantly and allow our wrong thinking to permeate our attitude toward people and circumstances.

As a result, we feel condemned ourselves and we condemn others for not being spiritually together enough to cope with difficult times when they come. We stamp "failure" all over people, including ourselves, when we should be "bearing one another's burdens."

If the strength of Christ was all we needed, then there would not be burdens for each other to bear. We would just be isolated, separate and self-contained believers with no need of each other. Come to think of it, isn't that just the way the church operates far too much of the time? Instead of being mutual supporters of each other, we abandon each other to a promise that is not a promise at all.

Equally unfortunate is the fact we deny each other the right to have emotions—as I am about to explain.

Jesus allowed the whole of His person, including His emotions, to respond in the way they were designed. The emotions He expressed were not marks of sin and failure. They were the normal outlet for someone overwhelmed by the situation He faced.

11
Can I Have My Emotions Back, Please?

In 1972, Senator Thomas Eagleton, riding on George McGovern's ticket, made a swift exit when it was disclosed he was being treated for depression. Sixteen years later Michael Dukakis walked away from his inquisitors, refusing to release medical records that would either prove or disprove he had twice undergone treatment for depression.

Such a negative attitude runs counter to the current American experience where, in 1987, 180,000 U.S. psychotherapists billed more than $2.5 billion in patient fees for practicing some 250 different types of therapy.

Our problem is we live under the shadow of a past generation who believed, "Big boys don't cry." And who considered displays of emotion "not nice." Such a shadow has also fallen on the Church. As a result, spiritual victory is too often regarded as having your emotions effectively subdued.

"Chin up and pull yourself together" was the order of the day for Christian disciples of past generations. It was taught in pulpits, conventions and books, leaving its mark indelibly on the way we now think and act. As a result, much of the Church today does not expect us to have emotions—except for those which reach heavenward. This is seldom spelled out in words—but it is an attitude continually implied by the actions of our fellow Christians.

Of course, we all *know* that emotions are an integral part of the way we are made. Our problem is that we all too easily lose sight of that fact and behave as though it were not true. We would never feel guilty over catching measles, pulling a calf muscle, needing to wear glasses or having our appendix burst. But, quite irrationally, we do not always enjoy the same clear conscience when our equally God-given emotions malfunction.

Can it really be that depression is sinful but diabetes is morally neutral? Why is it that mental illness is so often seen as a mark of sin and faithlessness when it occurs in Christians? As one who suffered commented, "We know only too well the side-long glances, the patronizing remarks, the spiritual exhortations, to which we are too often subjected; and they hurt."

Why is it okay to take medication to control blood pressure, ulcers, backache or angina, but not to give relief to mental and emotional anguish? As Dr. Marion Nelson declared in his classic but often unheeded book *Why Christians Crack Up,* published nearly thirty years ago, "The idea that a Christian can know perfect mental peace at every moment is unrealistic and unscriptural. The fact is that Christians can suffer from any medical or psychological disorders that affect the rest of mankind."[1]

Looking at Life in Two Dimensions

We are led to believe that something that is not physical must be spiritual. If it can be seen, it is physical. If it can't, it is spiritual. So if I break my leg, it is okay to limp. But if my heart is broken, and I "limp" emotionally, it is essentially a spiritual problem.

In our case, the answer to Rosemary's depression and stress was seen by the church leadership as her needing to pray more, come to church more, read her Bible more. The symptoms were emotional but the solutions offered were all spiritual.

Seeing that we faced an almost complete absence of practical help, one of our friends made the cynical suggestion, "Try breaking your leg. Then perhaps help will come." Rosemary did—and help did come. To be factual, she chipped an ankle bone. But at least a broken ankle could be seen and understood. People rallied round. The food began to arrive and someone even did the ironing.

That incident left Rosemary observing it would be better to be on kidney dialysis than to suffer from depression. At least people would believe there was something medically wrong and not write it off as having its root in either the imagination or in spiritual inadequacy.

Because we can control our thoughts, we assume that we—and others—ought to be able to control our emotions. And we grow frustrated and disillusioned when we fail. Worse still is when others expect us to respond to their encouragement, "Pull yourself together." In fact, that one phrase is the most thoughtless, cruel and unrealistic request anyone can make of someone operating under an

emotional cloud. If someone could pull themselves
together, then they most certainly would. No one wants to
wake up in the morning feeling as though some nocturnal
cosmic vacuum cleaner had sucked every last ounce of joy
from the universe. If there *was* a way in which someone
could feel different, then they would take hold of it with
both hands.

There will be those who are alarmed because I view
emotional distress as something that should be accepted
and responded to through a change in lifestyle and, when
necessary, professional caring channels. To some, depression and other stress-related conditions should be the
subject of spiritual warfare—to be rebuked and resisted.

There are times when this is true—but not often.
Gifted and perceptive counselors may very occasionally
recognize that either the symptoms have their root in hostile spiritual forces or divine healing is God's intention. But
innumerable unfortunate people, believing they should
have the same control over their feelings that they have
over their limbs, have been offered instant miraculous
release—only to be disappointed. They have incurred immense psychological damage as a result.

To those who insist on seeing every dark mood as
being ripe for prayers of healing and deliverance, I would
appeal for consistency. Torn ligaments do not induce
prayers for immediate healing and deliverance. Why should
emotional malfunctions be treated any differently? To do
so is dishonest and unbiblical. It could even be considered
malicious, because someone who remains unhealed from
mumps writes it off as "one of those things," while someone whose emotional condition stays unaltered tends to lay
the blame on themselves—adding even further to their
despair and lack of personal esteem.

Most of us would be more likely to do handstands

down the highway than we would to pray for instant deliverance from a broken leg. Yet we may find ourselves trapped into expecting instant and miraculous deliverance from symptoms of emotional stress. That goes to show how we *do* see those aspects of our makeup that are not visible as being "spiritual" rather than "emotional." Spiritually, we *can* move instantly from darkness to light, guilt to acquittal, resentfulness to forgiveness. But we put our emotions into the same camp when they do not belong there. Their place is alongside our physical entity, not our spiritual one. In effect, we are guilty of behaving as though God made humankind with only two dimensions — the physical and the spiritual.

The Source of Emotions

Even when we accept that emotions are valid, there can be uncomfortable assumptions about their source. This could not be more strongly expressed than through yet another advertisement that caught my eye in a Christian magazine. It asked ten questions which included, "Are you too tired or unable to cope?", "Do you have problems with depression, anxiety or fear?", "Do you have trouble concentrating or remembering?" The answer to these predominantly emotional problems was summed up in the headline of the advertisement which asked, "Could your problems be demonic in nature?" In other words, if there is something wrong with the way you feel, it could well be a spiritual issue.

The Bible shows that God has emotions — including anger, compassion, regret and sorrow. As we are all made in God's image we share those emotions too. Far from being sub-human to have emotions, it is a mark of complete normality.

The Bible reveals some of the greatest expressions

of human feeling through the psalmist David. We find him crying out in distress (Psalm 55:17), too troubled to speak (Psalm 77:4) and with a "heart wounded within me" (Psalm 109:22, NIV). He knew what it was to feel "downcast," "distressed within," "forgotten," in "mourning," and "oppressed" (Psalm 42).

The Lord Jesus proclaimed that those who experience the emotion of grief will be blessed. His promise was, "Blessed are those who mourn, for they will be comforted" (Matthew 5:4, NIV).

William Barclay tells us: "The word translated *mourn* is one of the strongest words for mourning in the Greek language. It is used for mourning for the dead." Barclay describes this grief as sorrow "which pierces the heart . . . a sorrow which is poignant . . . and intense."[2]

So Jesus is telling us that we should not see an outward display of emotions as an indication of inner spiritual inadequacy. He not only approves of emotions, but says that those who experience emotions of grief are blessed. We should not be surprised, because the Lord was no stranger to emotions Himself. At the tomb of Lazarus He was "deeply moved in spirit and troubled" (John 11:33, NIV) and He wept. This was not for some super-spiritual reason or as part of a pulpit performance. It was an expression of His humanness over the consummate grief that He felt for those who mourned the death of someone they loved. Nor was He play-acting when He was angry with the money changers in the Temple or when He wept over the city of Jerusalem.

Emotional Rights

If I am belaboring the point, it is because it needs to be. Too often I have seen the damage done through denying Christians the right to their emotions.

This is seen most clearly in our own attitude to grief. Not everyone of us will experience emotional distress through stress and trauma. But we all eventually face the death of someone we love. All too typical is the experience of a Christian couple who lost their fine teenage son in a car accident. When the news was shared with the church, it was announced that the couple "has been wonderfully victorious. Not a tear. Just rejoicing that God's sovereign will has been done and Brian is now in heaven which is far better." Nods of approval went round the church (the role model was at work). Affirmation was given to the belief that "victory" for the Christian means anaesthetizing your emotions.

This "don't grieve" idea may be due to a miunderstanding of Paul's words to the Christians in Thessalonica, where he told them, "We do not want you to be ignorant about those who fall asleep, or grieve like the rest of men, who have no hope" (1 Thessalonians 4:13, NIV). Paul is not giving instructions that the Thessalonians should not grieve. He is saying that their grief should be of a different kind to that shown by those who do not have any hope. Far from condemning grief, he is actually approving it. But he is calling for a grief filled with hope rather than despair.

The older you get the more you find yourself writing letters to those who have suffered bereavement. On those occasions I always encourage the recipient to try to see grief as a gift from God, the outlet provided by the Creator for us to express our sense of loss. If the emotion of love is a reality, then grief is its expression at the time of passing and separation. It is to us what a valve is to a pressure cooker. It is the release that is absolutely essential when our emotions are under pressure.

Several years ago I expressed this in a note to a

young woman grieving the loss of her much-loved grandfather. In a brief but heartfelt note of reply, she said, "Your letter arrived just when I needed it. I hadn't let myself cry. I guess I thought I needed to be strong, but I knew things were bottling up inside me. When I received your letter I felt such a release inside, and I was able to cry over the loss of someone I loved very much."

We're Not Alone

Just as we can find ourselves struggling to express the emotion of grief without feeling guilty or spiritually inadequate, so we can have the same problem over other emotions. It is essential to understand that it is truly valid for Christians to experience inner anguish, turmoil and pressure. This is not something reserved for the inadequate. A brief look at three major Old Testament prophets brings home a point we tend to miss: They also had emotions and encountered pressure points of their own.

We stand in awe of Moses leading the people out of Israel, crossing the Red Sea and receiving the Law from God. Yet we are blind to his self-pitying protests that the people's constant rebellion and seething discontent had worn him out. We fail to note his pleas to God that he had reached the limit of his resources, requesting to be "put to death right now" (Numbers 11:15).

Hearts rise to Elijah on Mount Carmel, calling down the fire of heaven and destroying 450 false prophets. But the following day that same spiritual giant is fleeing from the threats of one woman. Exhausted from his spiritual conquest and a day's sun-beaten journey across the desert, he shelters under a broom tree and prays, "I have had enough Lord. Take my life" (1 Kings 19:4, NIV).

The prophet Jonah is not much different. Once we

have the incident with the great fish behind us, we seem to progress no further than the triumph of his ensuing preaching crusade. But the sight of 120,000 people repenting in sackcloth and ashes led to an exhausted Jonah whose reputation and credibility was shot through. He had come to Nineveh warning that God would destroy the city. God had "let him down" by sparing the people. Jonah's response was the anguished cry, "It would be better for me to die than to live" (Jonah 4:8, NIV).

Emotions are part of our human make-up. Everyone is subject to them, including God's greatest servants. It could even be argued that those most committed to God are most at risk.

If you still need convincing, look no further than the Garden of Gethsemane. There, facing the greatest ordeal that the universe has ever seen, the Lord Jesus tasted those emotions Himself. As Mark records, "He began to be deeply distressed and troubled. 'My soul is overwhelmed with sorrow to the point of death,' he said to them" (Mark 14:33-34, NIV). That is some expression of emotion: "deeply distressed" and "overwhelmed with sorrow." But if the Lord had responded in the way that much of the Church demands of its people, He would have put on the Galilean equivalent of the stiff upper lip. He would have kept to the edict, "Don't let them see you cry."

Instead, Jesus allowed the whole of His person, including His emotions, to respond in the way they were designed. The emotions He expressed were not marks of sin and failure. They were the normal outlet for someone overwhelmed by the situation He faced. Jesus had no need to reproach Himself for the way He felt. Nor do we when distress, inner pain, sorrow and other similar responses arise as a result of the battles of life.

When our God-given emotions become subject to

stress—and misbehave accordingly—we have no more reason to feel guilty and condemned than we do over a pulled muscle. And we have every right to expect the Church to have the same attitude. Behaving as though we have no emotional dimension to our lives will rob us from ever finding peace under pressure.

To devote three chapters to the harm the Church can do to us really puts the pastors on the hotseat. Yet the truth is, they may be hurting even more than we are.

*Jesus treated leaders as having physical and human
needs. Too often we over-emphasize the supernatural
dimension of the lives of our leaders. Each leader is
expected to be an "Indiana Jones" of the ministry.*

12
What Are We Doing
to Our Leaders?

The Bible had been read; a prolonged time of worship
was over. Now it was time for some preaching. The cir-
cus-style big top was filled with close to 5,000 people. The
subject was "The Leadership of Christ," and I was the
speaker.

The evening was part of an event called Spring Harvest, which is probably the world's largest annual
inter-church Bible-teaching event. In major vacation
centers across the United Kingdom, more than 60,000
people of all ages gather during the Easter holiday. Present
are pastors and lay people, learning together.

Announcing my subject that night, I made a
promise, "This message is about leadership, but it is not for
leaders. I am here to speak on behalf of leaders. It is time
to understand how we are denying them the right to be the
kind of leaders that God wants, producing more hurt, stress

and pain for them than we can ever realize."

Forty minutes later, towels, washcloths and bowls of warm water were placed at points around the arena. "The hands of many of our leaders are hard and calloused, symbolically speaking, from the work they have done. They are also tired and in need of refreshment," I explained. "For those of you for whom it is appropriate, I invite you to take this opportunity and wash the hands of your pastor — ministering refreshment, love and commitment."

Within minutes, the vast crowd became a dynamic picture of the Christian life in action. Some formed natural small groups to pray for their leaders, repenting of the hurt and stress they had inflicted. Others washed hands, prayed, apologized, made fresh commitments. Many tears were shed; some whole churches experienced reconciliation, returning home with a new direction for the future.

I received a letter a few days later that was typical of the overwhelming response that came from the pastors present: "In my more than twenty years of pastoral ministry, I have never heard anyone address the needs of leaders as you did. It desperately needed saying. I only pray that my people who were there will understand and take action."

It was no surprise that the message proved so relevant. A survey of British clergy revealed that one in three had seriously considered leaving the ministry. I also knew the number of Church of England clergy taking early retirement had doubled over the past four years. A U.S. study of ex-pastors from the United Church of Christ showed that 68 percent expressed that leaving the ministry left them feeling happy, more free, more rewarded, more human, more secure and more satisfied.[1]

One United Kingdom denomination, the United

Reformed Church, issued a report suggesting that two out of three illnesses among ministers may be stress-related.[2] That same report quoted a denominational training college dean as saying that at least one in ten of that denomination's ministers may show evidence of stress "burnout." Another study revealed that one in three pastors have taken time out due to emotional/stress illness over the previous three years.[3]

Knowing all this, my task was to help the people I spoke to that evening see the difference between the kind of leadership that they desired and the kind that the Lord Jesus Christ modelled.

Leadership Is Human

Mark's record of the feeding of the 5,000 shows Jesus taking His disciples away after an exhaustive time of activity. The invitation was, "Come with me by yourself to a quiet place and get some rest" (Mark 6:31, NIV). The lesson is clear—Jesus treated leaders as having physical and human needs. Cut them and they bleed. Hurt them and they feel pain. Work them and they grow weary.

Yet, too often we over-emphasize the supernatural dimension of the lives of our leaders—their preaching, teaching, counseling and praying. Each leader is expected to be an "Indiana Jones" of the ministry. This is how *we* want them.

Our eyes are too often closed to the fact that Jesus took walks in a cornfield, enjoyed social meals, participated in a wedding, sailed a boat, rode a donkey, sang a hymn and cooked breakfast for His friends. Much of the pressure we inflict on our leaders stems from them being denied the same right to humanness.

Leaders Have Emotions

Matthew's account of the bread and fishes miracle places it immediately after Jesus receiving the news of the death of John the Baptist, one of His cousins. To quote, "When Jesus heard what had happened he withdrew by boat privately to a solitary place" (Matthew 14:13, NIV).

We see that the death of someone He loved brought Jesus emotional pain and loss. Jesus *felt* the death of John. Like our present-day leaders, He had emotions that could not be ignored.

I have already given examples of Jesus displaying His emotions. But note that we only know that Jesus expressed His emotions because His disciples were there to see it. He opened up His feelings to friends. Our leaders deserve that right as well. I am not recommending displays of emotional incontinence before whoever happens to be passing by, but our leaders need an inner group with whom they can be honest.

Leaders Face Pressure

Confronted with a huge and hungry crowd, Jesus turned to His disciples with the suggestion, "You feed them!" Ultimately, they failed the test and put Him under the kind of pressure we inflict on our leaders today.

"Send them away to solve their own problems" was the first proposal made by the disciples. There were no willing hands to ease the load. In our hurting world we all too often fail to be part of the solution – with the weight falling on the shoulders of the few who have the vision to make a difference. Leadership overload could be prevented if everyone played their part.

The disciples' second excuse was, "That would take

eight months of a man's wages" (Mark 6:37, NIV). The
disciples didn't deny they had the money. Their argument
was that it was an unreasonable request, simply too great
a level of self-sacrifice to contemplate. Could it even be that
for them to surrender eight months of wages to feed a crowd
would have been more of a miracle than the one Jesus was
eventually to perform? How painful for those with vision
who are torn apart by the complacency and lack of commitment from the rest of us.

In the fourth gospel, John adds yet another dimension to the saga by recording the pressure Jesus faced when
the miracle was over. Seeing the opportunity to enjoy free
food forever, the people "intended to come and make him
King by force" (John 6:15, NIV). They wanted Jesus for what
was in it for them.

Our own leaders are confronted by this same attitude. Those they serve are more concerned with receiving
than giving, with what they get than what they give. What
matters is their taste and their best interest—all are of
greater importance than what they can contribute. Small
wonder that our leaders are pressured.

Other Sources of Pressure

Yet all this is only a small part of the story. The
stresses and pressures that bear down on the leaders of our
churches come from a wide variety of sources. Many of the
key factors have been well defined by John Adams and Roy
Oswald of the Alban Institute.[4] They see them as—

Congregational Expectations. The congregation—
or sections within it—may have a different expectation of
the role that their minister should fulfill when compared
to his own game-plan. Or they may have unrealistic expectations of the range of gifts that any one person can have.
Or they may simply be wanting someone "just as wonder-

ful" as the last incumbent.

Unclear Job Descriptions. Those in "normal" employment benefit from clear job descriptions and well-defined channels of authority. Too many local church leaders — particularly those still stuck in the one-man-ministry rut — are expected to do "everything" and to be answerable to "everyone."

Such an inadequately defined role is likely to create a compulsive need to work even harder and harder in order to invoke the minimum amount of disappointment among those the leader is serving. That has to mean stress for anyone other than a sanctified Clark Kent.

Lack of Pastoral Care and Loneliness. It is a vast understatement to say that the pastoral care of the pastors is woefully inadequate. Only fellow ministers really understand the pressures. Yet professional masks are kept securely in place and stiff upper lips are never allowed to tremble in the presence of others.

The few structures that do exist in order to make mutual pastoral care possible tend to do little to take relationships beyond the superficial, as a fly on the wall of almost any minsters' fraternal meeting will tell you. The overall result is isolation and loneliness.

Economic Vulnerability. The generally low income of many pastors is a stress factor all its own. The guilt that comes from inflicting his family with the pressure of "the job" and from inadequate financial provision can be hard to carry. Added to that is the fact that the pastor's financial future and security is dependent on maintaining good relations within the church. Thus comes the stress of having to constantly look over his shoulder and listen for the distant hoofbeats of a vote of no confidence.

Time Demands. The pastor is never allowed to be

off duty. Even the most trivial of issues can occasion the words, "I knew I would find you in, Pastor, seeing it's your day off." There is also the interruption of emergencies. Some estimates indicate that 20 percent of a pastor's time is devoted to emergencies or the unexpected. Just when he is more or less successfully managing to juggle an already unrealistic workload, someone will lob in a few surprises and bring the lot crashing down.

Adams and Oswald were also able to create a stress-rating scale of their own, based on the ministers' evaluations of how true for them a number of statements are, including: "I must attend a meeting to get a job done"; "I get feedback only when my performance is unsatisfactory"; "I am fighting fires rather than working according to a plan"; "I am stuck with the responsibility when a volunteer doesn't follow through on a task"; "The congregation has role expectations for my spouse"; "I arrive at work in the morning without a clear picture of where to begin." These comments speak for themselves.

To the above we should add the observations of Enos D. Martin, an American psychiatrist, who has made a study of depression in the clergy.[5] He cites several reasons for pastoral depression:

Complex Role Expectations. A pastor has more expected of him than someone in any other profession. As well as being underpaid and overworked, he must be a theologian, philosopher, businessman, politician, educator, preacher, public relations expert and counselor. Yet his training is usually woefully inadequate in many of these areas. As a result, this complex set of expectations is matched by a sense of personal inadequacy.

Lack of Firm Roots. Moving from church to church is a standard procedure in ministry life—but it means losing the relationships which have become important to both the pastor and his family. It is a mark of the ministry that getting another pastorate just around the corner is simply "not done." The next job has to be a respectable distance away.

Unstructured Counseling. Other professionals with counseling responsibilities—psychiatrists for example—are able to work within a very structured setting. Their patients are seen for an agreed time and usually with a regular weekly time span between each contact. In contrast, the pastor can be called on at any hour of the day or night.

In addition, the minister is dealing with those about whom he cares deeply—and should he try to maintain a limit to this emotionally draining personal involvement, he can be accused of being uncaring.

Nowhere to Go. One of the major stress factors is that for a minister to go to a superior with his problems could lead to a question mark over his future. So he may just bottle it all up and struggle on.

In the United Kingdom, the United Reformed Church established a working party to produce their invaluable report "Stress in the Ministry," which echoed the findings of its American counterparts that we have considered.

The report also observes that pastors can be held hostage by the standards they set for others. Having established a "Christians don't have problems environment"—or inheriting one from the previous minister—they can face double trouble when problems become theirs. One pastor who had experienced depression is quoted as saying, "There were even a few [in my congregation] who had the idea that as a minister I had no right to feel depressed or anxious about anything, and that all I had to do was pray and God would sort out the hitch and, really, where was my faith?"[6]

The Leader's Family

If things sound bad for men in the ministry, it can be even worse for their wives. The same report calls attention to the distinctive pressures that a minister's wife has to face. These include—

The Expectations of Others. Church members and the public have their own "image" of what life in the parsonage should be like—and the wife has the pressure to fulfill those ideas.

Lack of Privacy. The husband and family are always on call. The needs of others must always be met even at the expense of the needs of the minister's own spouse.

Finance. It is not merely the problem of finding ways to cope on a low income that creates stress. It is also the issue of not feeling valued, together with the conflict between needing to be a homemaker and the pressure to take outside employment in order to make ends meet.

One minister's wife quoted in the report gives her own summary of the stress that she and her compatriots have to endure:

> The sense of isolation, lack of pastoral care either from the congregation or denomination, inadequate or badly maintained housing, unrealistic expectations and demands placed upon the minister, his wife and the family, and the heavy burden placed on the wives of ministers to provide the major financial support of the family—all place immeasurable stress upon the marriage relationship itself.

Emotional Needs. Clergy wives face the stress of their husbands spending extensive amounts of time in the company of other women — while they are at home feeling neglected and having to cope. Many a pastor comes home night after night too exhausted to meet the physical needs of his partner.

On the same theme, Shirley Dobson, wife and co-worker of Dr. James Dobson, sees the sexual stress in ministry marriages from another point of view. "Women need to be emotionally satisfied before they can be sexually satisfied," she explains. "But men in the ministry tend to be so busy and pre-occupied that their wives are emotionally neglected. So when it comes to lovemaking, their wives have a tendency to feel used, cheap and unfulfilled."

All these problems are compounded by the fact that, often, the one person a minister cannot pastor is his own wife. When there is an organized pastoral care scheme within the church, it is unlikely that the minister's family will be on anyone's list. And the family is inhibited from asking for help — it doesn't go with the role.

The stress that clergy wives face came to the surface when 400 wives of bishops attended the 1988 Lambeth Conference with their husbands. Sixty percent signed up for a workshop on the stress involved in living with a clergyman.

At the workshop was the wife of the Bishop of Manchester, Mrs. Anne Booth-Clibborn, a trained social worker. She says, "If you are a doctor's wife, people do not come to you for a prescription. But if you are married to a minister, you are expected to be a perpetual source of sympathy and concern."

We must also not overlook the children of our ministers who also pay the price. I am told on good authority that a pastor received a phone call from an irate church steward asking, "Why have all church meetings been cancelled?" Investigation revealed that a notice proclaiming that fact had been pinned to the church door. Further investigation disclosed that the "culprit" was the minister's son — who had not seen his father in weeks.

On reflection, I am surprised that this was an isolated incident. If someone were to manufacture "all meetings cancelled until further notice" notices, they could find a booming market among ministerial families — and maybe start a welcome trend!

Leaders Are Vulnerable

My fourth point, drawn from the miracle of the loaves and fishes, centers on the reason that Jesus set the whole incident in motion in the first place. Matthew records, "When Jesus landed and saw a large crowd, he had compassion on them and healed their sick" (Matthew 14:14, NIV). It was compassion that placed Him center stage in the drama of stress and pressure.

This reminds us that the qualities that make good pastors also put them at risk. A caring spirit, openness to others, sensitivity and empathy are actually the qualities that can make someone particularly vulnerable to the impact of stress. So pastors are not only subjected to excessive pressure points, but they are already particularly vulnerable to them as well.

Many of us never stop to consider that the way things are in our churches can create stress for those who have leadership responsibility within them. Tragically, our own lack of understanding then becomes yet another stress factor.

However bad all this sounds, please accept that it is actually worse than you might think. A poll of both pastors and lay people reveals that pastors are 50 percent more stressed over finance and 100 percent more stressed over their devotional life than their people imagine.[7]

Other areas where church members underestimate pastoral stress, according to the study, are time pressures, conflict issues, success pressures and housing. At the same time, the study shows that pastors are receiving only one-third of the level of support from their family that most members expect.

In her book "Coping With Stress at Work,"[8] Dr. Jacqueline Atkinson describes the symptoms of "burnout," the now well-accepted experience that hits mostly those in the caring professions. She lists the symptoms as including apathy, helplessness and hopelessness, overlaid with cynicism and possibly selfishness.

Dr. Atkinson points out that "most people who suffer burnout work within a bureaucratic organization . . . probably underfunded and usually subject to cuts; they may have low pay and/or status, work in isolation with little social support, have reached career plateau with little chance of advancement and, most importantly, be faced with demanding clients and no clear criteria of success or even task completion."

Does that sound like the ministry? Or does that sound like the ministry?

Dr. Atkinson adds that the most common response to burnout is to leave both the job and profession. This takes us back to almost the beginning of this chapter where we saw that eight out of ten who had left the ministry believe that they now have a better deal. Any of us with the power to affect the situation had better get to work — fast.

If we do not do something, we will be creating even more pressured pastors — like this one who wrote to me following my message on leadership. I'd like to conclude with his words:

> I am a minister and I came here on the edge of burn-out — physical, mental and spiritual. I was so bad off that I hadn't realized the problem. It was only on the second day, when attending your seminar on stress, that it dawned on me. Although the problem is still there, I have begun to get back in touch with God.
>
> The pressure had been so great. I had worked myself to a frazzle, teaching, leading, preaching, helping the Sunday School, playing the keyboards, leading the worship, running the house-groups, etc., etc., etc. A lot of it is my own doing and I now have some idea of the area where I must say no.
>
> What I am dreading is going home, to people who do not understand. I expect I am not the only leader here feeling guilty like this. I am just brave enough to admit it. So I pray that the members of my church who heard you speak on "The Leadership of Christ" last night will really take to heart that their leaders are human and do bleed — probably more easily than the rest of the members of the church. The problem is that we are so good at hiding it — often until it is too late.

Our circumstances do not tell us about God —
it is God who tells us about our circumstances.

13
Rejoice? Are
You Serious?

By reading this far, I hope you now understand where the pressure mortar bombs are likely to come from, why there are so many and why we are so often unable to cope. It is vital to accept that we *are* allowed to have problems and are *not* expected to cope with every dire circumstance. Yet, as Christians, we should also have clear understanding as to how God expects us to respond in order to find peace under pressure.

As those born into God's family, we are not subject to chance, luck or accidents. The God who rules the universe equally rules our lives. He does not arbitrarily inflict adverse circumstances upon us, but neither do such circumstances catch Him by surprise when they come. So how should we view them?

At the very moment I am writing these words, I should be at the silver wedding celebration of some great friends (who got married very young!). It would have been the first unhurried social night out for Rosemary and me in quite some time, and we had looked forward to it very much. Instead, I am in a hospital fifty miles from home and have just watched our fourth son, Zachary, return from surgery where they set his newly-broken arm. A mid-afternoon telephone call from the organizer of his Sunday school outing had prompted a swift drive and an equally speedy change of plans.

When the news gets out, we will face the usual ribald taunts as to whether our family has shares in plaster of paris — seeing that this is the third arm to be broken (all different children!) in less than nine months. The previous two came within three days of each other.

But what are we to make of stress-inflicting circumstances like these? How are we to respond when the world or the church lays yet another straw on our back?

What God Expects of Us

It is in providing an answer to those questions that I find myself in danger of losing you as a reader — because God's instructions to those faced with the trials of life seem to be totally unrealistic. So unrealistic that, as I share them with you, you could find yourself saying, "Who are you kidding?" and switch off completely to what follows.

What does God expect of us? Try this for size: *Joy.* Or to express it more fully, "Consider it pure joy, my brothers, whenever you face trials of many kinds" (James 1:2, NIV).

Can you cope with that? The dog has just chewed the new carpet; the twins have mumps; something sneaked into the wash and turned everything pink; and here comes a fanatic apostle called James, yelling "Rejoice!" How unrealistic can you get?

Yet it *is* realistic—just like everything else in the Bible. God is telling us that willfully to exercise joy in the face of adversity is the only adequate response we can make.

Yes, I know that sounds ridiculous. But before you throw it out, allow me to explain exactly *why* it is that James would have us respond to our trials with joy. Unreasonable as it seems, if you can shelve your objections until you understand James's motivation, it can bring a completely new dimension to your life and help to deliver you from the resentment and confusion that too often accompanies such experiences.

What Is Meant by Trials?

First we must put the command to "rejoice when all kinds of trials come our way" into its context. A very bad accident, the death of someone close, redundancy, serious ill health—none of these are "trials," unless you are incredibly thick-skinned and insensitive. These are all tragedies and it is not to events like these that James asks us to respond with outbursts of joy.

There are also events which most people may see as being merely a trial, but to us they are a disaster. It may be that these incidents either have some special significance or simply are the last straw. James does not call us to meet these events with joyfulness either. Such happenings bring forth the weeping that enables others to weep with us. So while we may, at first sight, view James's instruction as being unrealistic, at least we can see that he is not advocating masochism.

A "trial" could be defined as a stone in the shoe of life—a circumstance that brings pressure and disorder without leaving us overwhelmed.

132   *PEACE UNDER PRESSURE*

Why should we respond to trials with joy?

There Is a Purpose

James says, "Consider it pure joy . . . because . . . the testing of your faith develops perseverance. Perseverance must finish its work so that you may be mature and complete, not lacking anything" (James 1:2-4, NIV). The trials that come to us have a role to play, James is telling us. They have a reason and a purpose. They are to create the mature qualities of "stickability" and wholeness of character.

Not that each individual irritation is hand-picked by God in order to promote the fruit He desires. He does not plot and plan to bring frustrations to us. It is just that pressures and adverse circumstances—the stuff that real life is made of—contribute to making us into more balanced and complete people.

The old Arab proverb puts it beautifully: "All sunshine makes a desert." Certainly the most immature and "barren" personalities are those who have sailed through life with the sun always shining. In contrast, those for whom life has been a struggle tend also to be the ones to whom others reach out for when their own struggles come. They reach out with a confident expectation that they will be understood because someone has been there before and gained experience and maturity in the process.

We should rejoice, James is telling us, because there will be a glorious end result—the completeness of our character.

There Is Future Reward

It is one thing to have a more complete character

here and now; it is quite another to receive a special reward when life is over. This is what James is also promising. He explains, "Blessed is the man who perseveres under trial, because when he has stood the test, he will receive the crown of life that God has promised to those who love him" (James 1:12, NIV).

One of the marks of someone heading for a future life with God is that they persevere under trial. When we see ourselves hanging tough in the face of adversity, it should cause us to be joyful, because this is the evidence that we are on the right road. At some later point, in a twinkling of an eye, we will find ourselves on the winner's dais, the national anthem of heaven playing, and the medals of victory will be ours.

We rejoice because trials give us the opportunity to affirm that our feet are on the road to heaven.

God Does Not Change

When circumstances turn for the worse, our reflex action is often to feel that God has changed too. He is somehow less loving, less committed to us, less benevolent than He was when things were good. That is not how it is. James insists that God "does not change like shifting shadows" (James 1:17, NIV). In effect, our circumstances do not tell us about God — it is God who tells us about our circumstances.

However bleak events may be, we cannot interpret them as telling us that God has ceased to be the loving, all-powerful, fair and extravagant heavenly Father that He is. Instead, because He is like that, it means our difficulties are in His control and His purposes for us are good.

God does not change. There is no danger that we may wake up one morning and find that He is no longer holy, just and good. Or that He feels vindictive and cruel. The Christian knows that God will never behave out of character. And we know what that character is like. James tells us, "The Lord is full of compassion and mercy" (James 5:11, NIV). This is the stuff our heavenly Father is made of, even though the clouds of circumstances may hide that shining fact from us.

When fair winds are blowing in our direction, we have no problem in recognizing what God is really like. I was present for the birth of each of our five children. Words can never express how good Rosemary and I felt God to be on every occasion. You can probably recall similar moments when God has seemed overwhelmingly good. He remains *that* good even when circumstances are not. He was still *that* good at the moment I hung up the telephone from speaking to the secretary of Rosemary's doctor, having been left with the belief that my life partner had only months to live.

No matter what befalls us or how high adversities pile up, the truth is that, in those moments, we are loved to the same extravagant extent as when the Lord Jesus gave His life for us on the cross. Our Lord is the same yesterday, today and forever. What He was yesterday, He is today and will be tomorrow – no matter what trials are ours.

Having a God like that is why rejoicing is in order.

Sitting here, in a strange hospital, with a child swathed in plaster, I must confess to finding myself somewhat less than joyful. Just contemplating sleeping on a cot in the corner of a children's ward – compared with the comforts of home – is enough to stir up a tidal wave of self-pity. But I do know that the willful expression of joy is what I should be aiming at – however short of that target I may fall.

James asks us to *decide* to rejoice. It is not something that is an automatic work of God's Spirit within us. If it were, James would not have needed to instruct his fellow Christians to respond to their trials with joy. And the fact that he had to give this instruction shows they were not making a decision to do so. So if you see yourself as being deficient in the "rejoicing in trials" department, then you are in good company. The first Christians were not doing any better.

At those awful moments, when the mind is too numb to evaluate what is happening, I have discovered only one supreme source of comfort—the Lord Jesus has experienced what I am experiencing.

14
When All Else Fails, Hang on to Dad

Despite all the attempted wisdom and insight strewn across the preceding pages, I have to admit that there may be times when it is of no value at all. Such a time may not be the experience of everyone, but it may be for you or someone close to you.

Circumstances can become so engulfing that nothing makes sense anymore and your brain is too battered to wrap itself around the theory of why you feel the way you do. It makes little difference whether you've reached this point because of one stark monumental hammer blow or a continued relentless barrage of adversity when the light at the end of the tunnel always turns out to be a train heading straight for you. The result can be the same—an inability to understand or respond with any sense of hope or purpose.

Rosemary and I have both faced situations like that

at different times and in different ways. Many a tear has been shed as we met wave after wave of illness, misunderstanding, rejection and misadventure. Trouble in a dozen shapes and sizes has made its way to our door. At times we have been bruised, bewildered and battered to the point of almost despairing of life itself.

It is true that what we have been through is nothing compared to the multitudes who have encountered crippling accidents, financial disasters, fatal diseases or loss of livelihood. Yet there is very little comfort, at a time of immense personal crisis, in having the head knowledge that there are thousands worse off than you. Perhaps it should help, but it turns out to be cold comfort when the heat is on. You may even find yourself feeling guilty for not being able to cope when there are others worse off than yourself.

At those awful moments, when the mind is too numb to evaluate what is happening, I have discovered only one supreme source of comfort—the Lord Jesus has experienced what I am experiencing. And the answer He found is enough for me too.

Come with me again to the Garden of Gethsemane. There we find the Lord "deeply distressed and troubled... overwhelmed with sorrow to the point of death" (Mark 14:33-34, NIV). So great is His anguish that sweat like great drops of blood falls from His brow. However great my own inner turmoil and distress may be, I know that my Savior can do more than sympathize from a distance. He can empathize because He has been through it all—and more.

The Lord Jesus has felt the pain of being abandoned, betrayed, exploited and pushed to the limits. He is not left trying to imagine what it must be like to be me when I am emotionally overrun. His own experience tells Him exactly what it is like.

But even grasping the truth of that amazing statement may not be enough to see us through — and it doesn't have to be the limit of our resources. The response that Jesus made in His own hour of darkness is the ray of hope that can see us through as well.

There in the garden Jesus says, "Abba, Father" (Mark 14:36). That one word — *Abba* — sums up the key to our survival. That simple Aramaic word means "Daddy."

The Lord Jesus had already brought a new revelation about God to those who heard Him. Until then they only understood God as the Father of their nation. Now Jesus spoke of God as a Father to individuals. But He reserves His own most intimate expression of His father-child relationship for His moment of greatest anguish.

We could be forgiven for imagining that the opposite would be the case. That it would have been moments of great spiritual ecstasy or triumph that ushered in such childlike abandon. On the Mount of Transfiguration, for example, or at the raising of Lazarus from the dead. But it is not so.

It is alone on a hillside, struggling with His whole destiny, that Jesus falls into the language of the nursery. Distressed, troubled, sorrowing to the point of death, Jesus responds with the word that He first spoke with dribble running down His chin: "Daddy."

That childlike expression, when spoken to God, expresses the simplest yet deepest truth that can be told. It was Father God who brought us to life by an act of His love. It is Father God who cherishes us with an overwhelming love. It is Father God whose plans for us are always in our best interest.

Circumstances may try to cloud the issue. But God is still "Abba, Father" and worthy to be trusted with our bewilderment and doubt. In my own Gethsemane moments my response has been, "Father, I know You are here somewhere. I cannot see You, feel You or sense Your presence. But You are a loving heavenly father – and fathers do not abandon their children. So I am just going to keep on keeping on until the mists have cleared and I can see You again." God expects no more of us than that.

It is the nature of a child not always to understand the reasons that fathers do things or allow them to happen. A recognition that God is "Daddy" helps to bring that fact into focus. On one terrible African night, missionary Helen Roseveare was raped and almost killed. In the days that followed, with the word *why* reverberating in her head, it seemed the Lord came to her and said, "Helen, can you thank me for trusting you with this experience even if I never explain why?"

We tend to assume that everything can be explained, that we would be capable of understanding if only God would take the trouble to tell us. Yet supposing some things *are* beyond our comprehension, that God is denied the opportunity to explain because it is not within our ability to grasp the meaning of what He would say.

Of all the traumas that have befallen our children, the one that haunts me the most concerns our third son, Aran, when he was about five years old. Running across our backyard at his frenetic speed, he tripped. Head and garden bench collided, badly tearing the corner of Aran's eyelid. One glance confirmed it needed stitches and we made our familiar route to the emergency room.

The necessary stitches required a local anaesthetic, but the injection did not allow him to look the other way. The result was an agonizing ten minutes while I physically held Aran down in order for the essential treatment to take place. There, wrapped in my arms and fighting tenaciously, his very best interests were being served. From his fearful and confused perspective, I was contributing to his pain. All he could say was "Daddy" as we both cried together.

That is a picture of the way it has been, or will be, for many of us. If we could only see things from a different angle, we would find that God did know what He was doing, even though it made no sense to us. We would also see we were fully engulfed in His loving embrace. He was not sympathizing from a distance, but personally and intimately involved in our experience.

For many of us, the heart of our failure to find peace under pressure is because we fail to grasp that we have a loving heavenly Father—who cares.

If we could see things from the perspective of heaven, perhaps we would even observe that we are not the only ones crying.

There are also tears in the eyes of the Father.

Notes

Chapter 2

1. *Newsweek* (April 25, 1988), pp. 28-33.
2. Of course there are reasons why someone may suffer from depression other than by racking up too high a score on the stress chart. Depression can have its root in changes in the body that have no link with stress. Or it can stem from a deep emotional response to some significant loss.
3. Based on T. H. Holmes and R. H. Rahe, "The Social Readjustment Rating Scale," *Journal of Psychosomatic Research*, II, 1967, pp. 213-218.

Chapter 3

1. Edward de Bono, *Dictionary of Vital Words* (London: Pierrot Publishing, 1977).

Chapter 4

1. Gordon MacDonald, *Restoring Your Spiritual Passion* (Nashville, TN: Thomas Nelson, 1986), p. 29.
2. Daniel M. Kehrer, "How to Cut Debt," *Changing Times* (April 1988), pp. 23-24.

Chapter 5

1. Ron Hutchcraft, *Peaceful Living in a Stressful World* (Nashville, TN: Thomas Nelson, 1985).

Chapter 7

1. Dr. Desmond Kelly, "Fit to Cope With Stress?" *The Times,* London (June 8, 1989), p. 14.

Chapter 8

1. Richard Young, "Stress Makes or Breaks the Man," *Sunday Times,* United Kingdom (March 27, 1988).

2. Dr. Paul Bevington appearing in an interview on *Stress*, a six-part series by HTV, Wales (April/May 1988).

3. Quoted in "Working Can Be a Health Hazard," *Sunday Times, United Kingdom* (February 24, 1985).

4. *Newsweek*, (April 25, 1988). p. 32.

5. Quoted in "Stress Makes or Breaks the Man," *Sunday Times,* United Kingdom (March 27, 1988).

6. Reported in *International Management* (May 1984).

Chapter 9

1. *Does church commitment put your family under pressure?*

	Up to 5 yrs	Up to 10 yrs	Up to 20 yrs	Up to 30 yrs	Over 30 yrs
Yes	63%	54%	49%	46%	26%
No	37%	46%	51%	54%	74%

Family Marriage Survey conducted by *Family* (now *Christian Family*) magazine, United Kingdom (October 1980).

2. Gavin Reid, "There Seems to be No Way of Escape," *Family* (now *Christian Family*) magazine, United Kingdom (February 1981).

3. *Does church commitment put your family under pressure?*

	Under 25	25-34	35-44	45-54	Over 55
Yes	60%	58%	46%	38%	42%
No	40%	42%	54%	62%	58%

Another important factor that should influence our priorities in pastoral care arises from the results of this survey. The following table indicates the four major areas of stress according to length of marriage. Let he who has eyes read—and respond.

	Up to 5 yrs	5-10 yrs	10-20 yrs	23-30 yrs	Over 30 yrs
1	Church	Finance	Discipline Children	Sex	Sex
2	Finance	Church	Finance	Relationships	Relationships
3	Relationships	Sex	Church	Children*	Finances*
4	Sex	Relationships	Sex	Finance*	In-Laws*

*equal

4. Gordon MacDonald, *Restoring Your Spiritual Passion* (Nashville, TN: Thomas Nelson, 1986), p. 31.

5. Gordon MacDonald, *Ordering your Private World* (Nashville, TN: Thomas Nelson, 1984), p. 42.

Chapter 11

1. Dr. Marion Nelson, *Why Christians Crack Up* (Chicago: Moody, 1967 rev), p. 5.

2. William Barclay, *The Plain Man Looks at the Beatitudes* (Glasgow, Scotland: William Collins and Sons, Fount, 1977), p. 25.

Chapter 12

1. G. Jud, E. Mills and G. Burch, *Why Men Leave the Parish Ministry* (Philadelphia: Pilgrim Press, 1970).

2. "Stress in the Ministry," London report by the United Reformed Church, 1987.

3. Keith Roberts, "Pressure Points: Stress Survey," *Today,* United Kingdom (March 1989).

4. John Adams and Roy Oswald, "Ministry Related Stress," *Leadership* (Winter Quarter 1984), p. 95.

5. Enos D. Martin, "Depression and the Clergy," *Leadership* (Winter Quarter 1982), p. 80.

6. "Stress in the Ministry," London report by the United Reformed Church, 1987, p.6

7. Keith Roberts, "Pressure Points: Stress Survey," *Today,* United Kingdom (April 1989), p. 40.

8. Dr. Jacqueline Atkinson, *Coping With Stress at Work* (London: Thorsons, 1988), p. 21.

Bibliography

Books/Publications

Adair, John. *How to Manage Your Time*. Talbut Adair, 1988.

Atkinson, Jacqueline M. *Coping With Stress at Work*. Thorsons Publishing Group, 1988.

Back, Ken and Kate. *Assertiveness at Work*. McGraw-Hill, 1982.

Coleman, Doctor Vernon. *Overcoming Stress*. Sheldon Press, 1988.

Davies, Gaius. *Stress*. Kingsway, 1988.

Dickson, Anne. *A Woman in Your Own Right — Assertiveness and You*. Quartet, 1987.

Galer, Anne and Pratt, D. Alasdair. *Stress in the Ministry*. United Reformed Church, 1987.

Horsman, Sarah. *Living With Stress — A Guide for Christian Ministers*. Society of Mary and Martha, 1987.

Jones, Doctor Alfred. *Stress Management*. Stress Control Products Ltd, 1988.

Nelson, Marion H. *Why Christians Crack Up*. Moody, 1967.

Selye, Hans. *The Stress of Life*. McGraw-Hill, 1956, revised ed., 1976.

Toffler, Alvin. *Future Shock*. Random House, Inc., 1970.

Articles

Adams, John and Oswald, Ron. "Ministry-related Stress," *Leadership,* Winter quarter, 1980.

Ahlbom, A., Baker, D., Karasek, R. A., Marxer, F. and Theorell, T. "Job Decision Attitude, Job Demands and Cardiovascular Disease: A prospected study of Swedish men. Am. J.

Public Health 71:694-705, 1981.

Breecher, Mawry M. "Six Ways to Get Un-depressed," *Complete Woman,* 1988.

Cirsta, Alix. "Relax! A Positive Approach to Stress," *Woman's Journal* (UK), August 1988.

Grice, Elizabeth. "Stress Makes or Breaks the Man," *Sunday Times*, March 27, 1988.

Jones, Michael. "The Stressed Doctor in a Stressful Society," General of the Christian Medical Fellowship (UK), April 1988.

Land, Barbara. "Fit to Cope with Stress?" *The Times*, June 8, 1989.

Levoy, Gregg. "Tears that Speak," *Psychology Today,* July 1988.

Littleton, Mark R. "Depression: The Chemical Side," *Moody Monthly,* October 1981.

Martin, Enos D. "Depression in the Clergy," *Leadership,* Winter quarter, 1984.

McBride, Michael G. "The Vocational Stress of Ministry," *Ministry*, January 1989.

McBride, Michael G. "Managing Ministerial Stress," *Ministry,* March 1989.

Moss, Professor Rowland. "Stress and Depression—A Personal Experience," *Christian Arena*, June 1984.

Overstreet, R. Larry. "After the Funeral," *Moody Monthly,* May 1981.

Roberts, Keith. "Pressure Points/Stress Survey," *Today,* March 1989.

Roberts, Keith. "A View from the Pews/Stress Survey," *Today,* April 1989.

Tucker, Ruth A. "Working Mothers," *Christianity Today*, July 15, 1988.

"Stress on the Job," *Newsweek,* April 25, 1988.

Index

Help for People Who Are Hurting

Quantity		Total
___	**FREEING YOUR MIND FROM MEMORIES THAT BIND** *by Fred & Florence Littauer.* Setting forth a biblical basis for inner healing through Jesus Christ, the authors explore emotional dysfunction and the childhood experiences which potentially lead to it. ISBN 0-89840-232-2/$8.95	$_____
___	**ROSES IN DECEMBER** *by Marilyn Willett Heavilin.* Written by a mother who lost three sons, this book offers practical, sensitive advice for those who are grieving. A bestseller! ISBN 0-89840-171-2/$7.95	$_____
___	**DECEMBER'S SONG** *by Marilyn Willett Heavilin.* This sequel to **ROSES IN DECEMBER** offers hope to the grieving and gives helpful, sensitive advice for both lay and professional caregivers. ISBN 0-89840-210-7/$7.95	$_____
___	**GOD IS NOT FAIR: Coming to Terms With Life's Raw Deals** *by Joel A. Freeman.* Sensitive, positive help for all who may feel or say, "God Is Not Fair." A popular, humorous style that introduces readers to the sovereignty of God. ISBN 0-89840-189-5/$6.95	$_____

Indicate product(s) desired above. Fill out below.
Send to:

HERE'S LIFE PUBLISHERS, INC.
P. O. Box 1576
San Bernardino, CA 92402-1576

NAME_____

ADDRESS_____

STATE_____ZIP_____

☐ Payment (check or money order only) included
☐ Visa   ☐ Mastercard #_____

Expiration Date_____Signature_____

ORDER TOTAL $_____

SHIPPING and
HANDLING $_____
($1.50 for one book, $0.50 for each additional. Do not exceed $4.00.)

APPLICABLE
SALES TAX (CA, 6%) $_____

TOTAL DUE $_____

PAYABLE IN U.S. FUNDS.
(No cash orders accepted.)

FOR FASTER SERVICE CALL TOLL FREE:
1-800-950-4457

FPU 276-X

Your Christian bookstore should have these in stock. If not, use this "Shop-by-Mail" form.
PLEASE ALLOW 2 TO 4 WEEKS FOR DELIVERY.
PRICES SUBJECT TO CHANGE WITHOUT NOTICE.

BUILDING BETTER FAMILIES

Practical Resources
to Strengthen Your Home

Quantity   Total

____ **FAMILY FITNESS FUN** *by Charles Kuntzleman.* $_____
Enjoy the sense of freedom that comes with feeling
healthier and more energetic by tapping into this
hassle-free handbook to a wholesome family lifestyle.
A book for the entire family with over 180 stimulating
strategies and activities for both parents and children.
ISBN 0-89840-279-4/$9.95

____ **HELPING YOUR KIDS HANDLE STRESS** *by H.* $_____
Norman Wright. Whether your child is a toddler or
teen, the author offers practical ways to spot a stress
problem, identify its source, and help your child learn
to cope with stress successfully.
ISBN 0-89840-271-9/$7.95

____ **PULLING WEEDS, PLANTING SEEDS: Grow-** $_____
ing Character in Your Life and Family *by Dennis*
Rainey. An inspiring collection of pointed reflections
on personal and family life with an abundance of practical insights for everyday living.
ISBN 0-89840-217-4/hardcover, $12.95

____ **MOM AND DAD DON'T LIVE TOGETHER** $_____
ANYMORE *by Gary and Angela Hunt.* Help and encouragement for youth and their parents who are
working through this confusing time. If a divorce has
happened in your family, your kids need to know that
they are not alone—or wierd—and that there is hope
for their future. ISBN 0-89840-199-2/$5.95

____ **TALKING WITH YOUR KIDS ABOUT LOVE,** $_____
SEX AND DATING *by Barry & Carol St. Clair.* The
topic which strikes fear in the heart of every parent!
Learn to resolve your fears and build an atmosphere
of love, trust and ongoing interaction with your kids
on these vital topics. ISBN 0-89840-241-7/$7.95

____ **THE DAD DIFFERENCE: Creating an Environ-** $_____
ment for Your Child's Sexual Wholeness *by Josh*
McDowell and Dr. Norm Wakefield. Sets the stage for
fathering that will dramatically improve parent/teen
relationships and reduce teen sexual excesses. Practical examples of role modeling and father/children activities. ISBN 0-89840-252-2/$8.95

(Continued on next page.)